ELVIRA
ESPEJO AYCA

KIRKI QHAÑI
CONTAINER OF ANDEAN POETICS

INCA

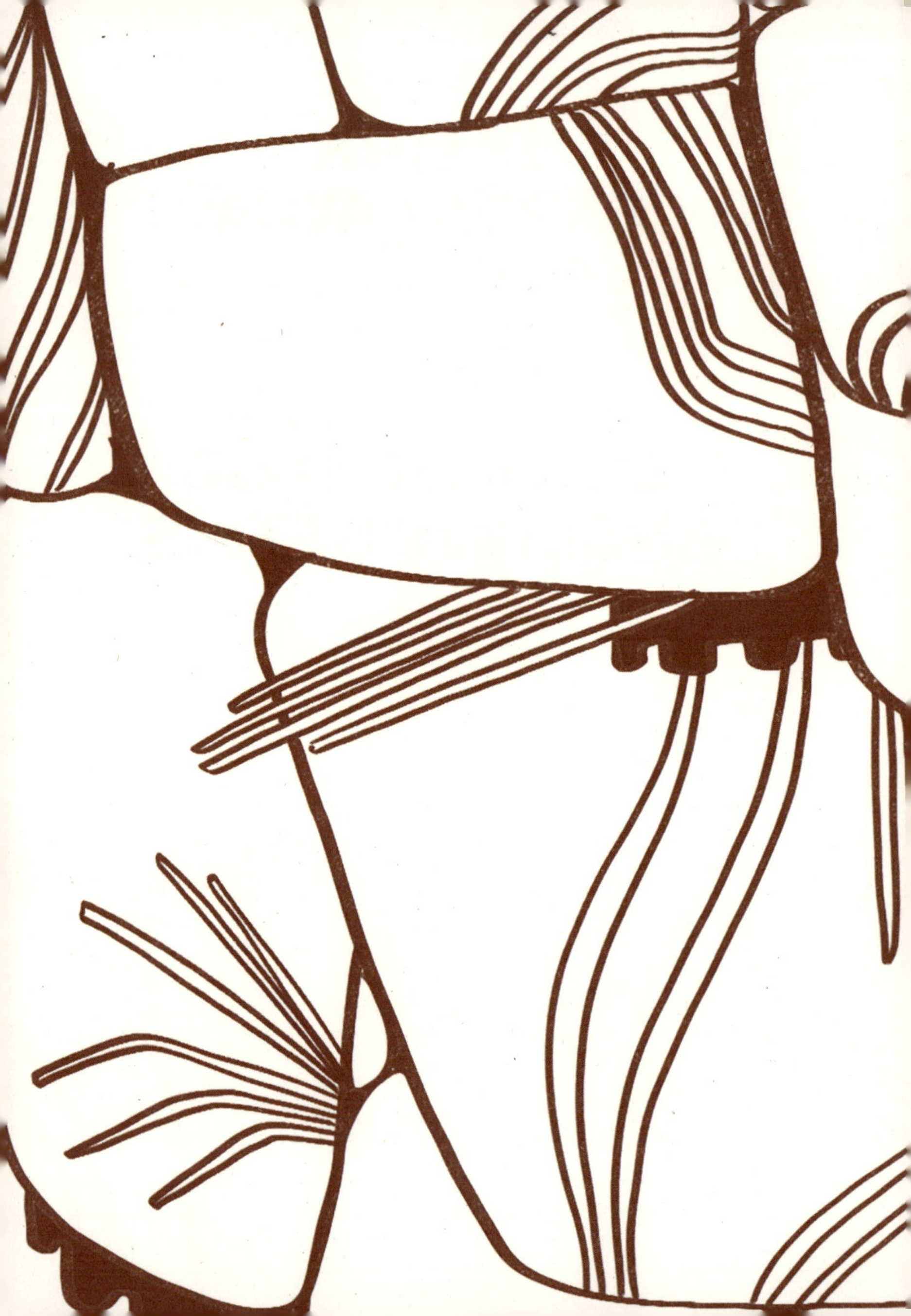

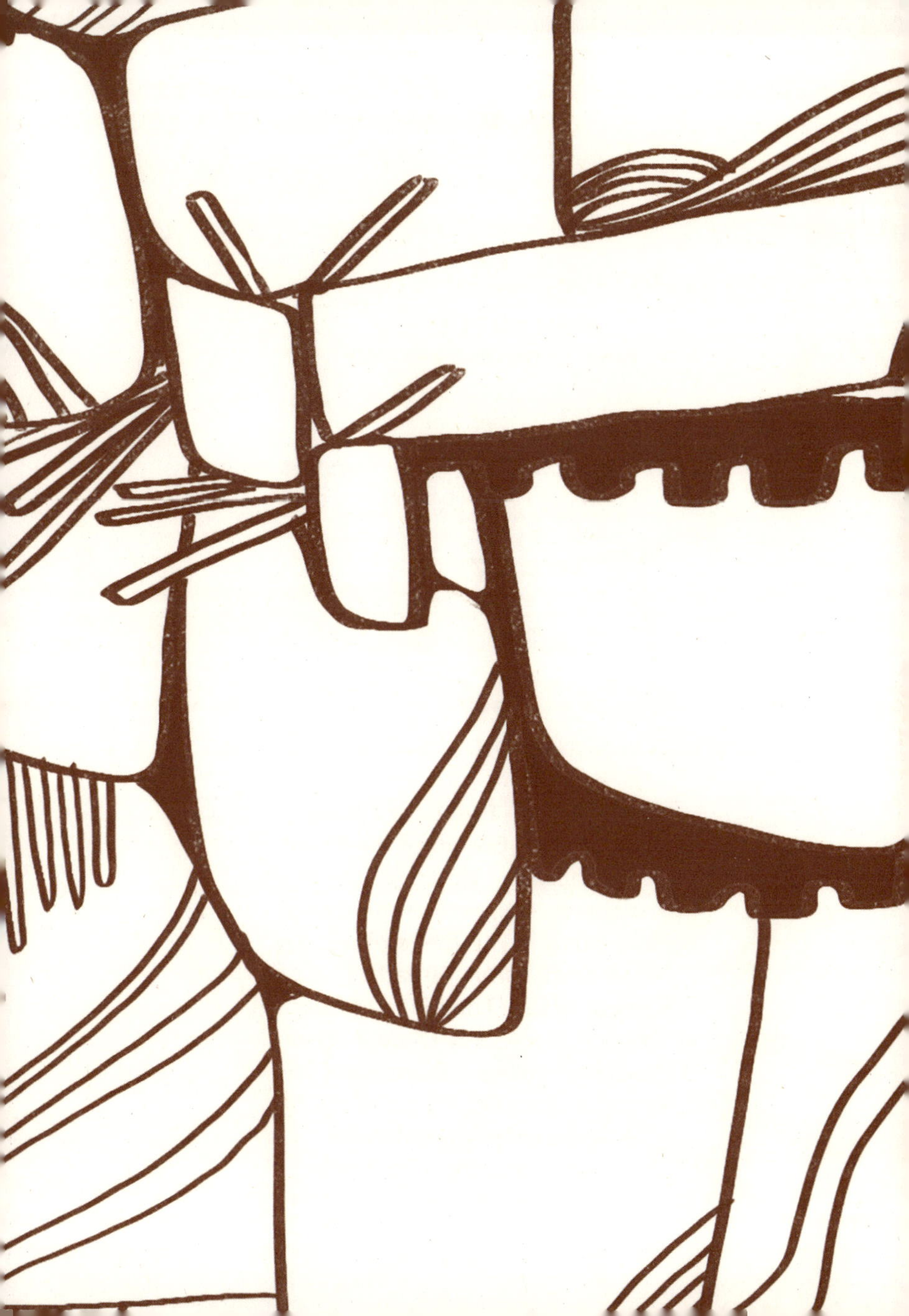

TRANSLATORS' INTRODUCTION

Aeron Bergman and Alejandra Salinas

Communication has always been the essential challenge in the stretching, isolated regions of the Andes mountains. Despite great distances and brutally rugged terrain, Andean people built incredibly successful, coherent, and mutually beneficial societies, that have lasted through time and hardship. Methods of spreading culture and knowledge are diverse, but one of the most important ways involve ritual. Due to several factors, Andean pre-Columbian societies have not relied on the written word to transmit information, instead perfecting a biological archive where knowledge of the essentials of civilization from agriculture, architecture, infrastructure, literature, and law were packaged in ritual forms, rites and actions. Especially valuable are its songs and oral language transmissions, thusly wrapped into cosmological narratives from their origins. It is notable that the original language of the song/poems in this book is Aymara, however Quechua, Spanish, and other language threads are woven within, containing the history of the Andean people. The song/poetry in this book reaches far, far back into this Andean tradition.

Elvira Espejo Ayca learned these song/poetry rituals in her *Ayllu*, and concretely from her grandmother Gregoria Mamani Sirqi. *Ayllu* is a word both in Aymara and Quechua that refers to a self-sufficient, self-governing, traditional form of living, something between a village and a family unit, formed by reciprocal relations. *Ayllus* existed as chains of communities stretching the entire length of the Andes, forming long before the Inca, and holding strong even after the tragic arrival of the Spanish. This chain continues but is no longer unbroken in modernity, as many young people are no longer recipients of their ancestral knowledge: the cultural information held within this chain is in danger of being lost. This is especially acute in the growing cities where the urge to be international exerts increasing pressure to leave the past further behind.

The remediation of ritual forms and oral traditions into a book form is also an act of translation. Espejo Ayca has long been engaged in the urgency of this project: as director of the National Museum of Ethnography and Folklore in La Paz, she completely re-imagined the museum as an accessible, ordered, but innovative space of knowledge to ensure as much as possible from the chain of knowledge survives. Her work also as an artist, singer, storyteller, and weaver provides the fullest possible context for the culture of the Andean community: for the full genius of the traditions to be carefully scaffolded for building the future. Espejo Ayca's work is a contemporary art practice that reframes indigeneity as the stubborn rebellion of continued existence, in opposition to the powerful gravity of global homogeneity and the art world's norms of stylistic novelty.

We began working on this book with Espejo Ayca first by translating to English the song/poems she herself had translated to Spanish from the original Aymara. It however became quickly apparent that the most important words could not be simply translated from Aymara into English without shedding almost everything from their context that makes them rich. We talked through this challenge for over a year. In La Paz, Espejo Ayca invited us to her favorite lunch spot a short walk downhill from the museum in the *Casco Urbano Central* of the incredible city built in the sweeping valley between mountain peaks. Walking through the lively *Mercado Lanza*, Espejo Ayca guided us past stalls selling a hundred varieties of potato, freshly baked bread, and small family kitchens serving up steaming plates from every region of Bolivia. She finally led us to her favorite spot: a tiny kitchen made up of a bench of hot pots preparing plates of *Ají de papa*: a bed of stewed potatoes and large starchy corn, topped with fried lake trout and small *ispi* fish with yellow and red *aji* spice, from *Lake Titicaca*, the sacred lake of the Andes.

Over this simple but profoundly nourishing traditional meal, we agreed that to transmit essential information we should keep as much Aymara as possible. Rather than attempting to smooth the text through roughly translated English, we decided that we would build a glossary with fuller descriptions of the symbols and layers sedimented within each term, located in footnotes and as columns located at the end of the book.

After our meal we spent a long afternoon drinking Bolivian coffee in her cozy, sun-streaked office in a quiet corner of the National Museum of Ethnography and Folklore. Under sweeping views of the mountains, working through four languages, our daughter Agnes lifted her head occasionally from her stack of books and drawings to join the conversation, lost in fascination. How wonderful that *chullumpi* refers to wave patterns in the water formed by movements of the fabled *chullumpi* bird (known as the grebe in English) that poetically also refers to patterns formed by wind blowing through fluffy llama fur! How are these symbolic meanings carried through time? How do we convey this richness into English?

Later, we included Adrian Alarcón whose experience working with Espejo Ayca ensured the Aymara was reflected sincerely, and he sharpened numerous moments in the text. We also included Max Jorge Hinderer Cruz in the conversations, an esteemed colleague who has worked with Espejo Ayca in past projects.

We incorporated texts in the languages they were originally written, Aymara or Spanish, followed by their respective translations to English.

This work of translation involved at least six people; it was therefore a collaboration in the spirit of the song/poetry contained in this book. It is through collaboration that the Andean people built incredibly improbable roads through mountain ridges and deserts connecting isolated *Ayllus* through time, creating interlinking chains of people that formed one of the most important human civilizations in history that continues to unfold, surprise, and offer guidance on potential futures. The depth of knowledge and richness of the Andean people is slowly being translated and transcribed into exhibitions, and books such as this one.

It is our honor to form part, in a small way, of this chain.

We would also like to thank and acknowledge Salvador Pomar for the lovely drawings throughout, as well as El Cuervo Editorial in La Paz, who in 2022 published the Spanish translation of this book.

Columbia, Missouri, 2025

ELVIRA ESPEJO AYCA: *KIRKI QHAÑI* *CONTAINER OF ANDEAN POETICS*

Max Jorge Hinderer Cruz

Elvira Espejo Ayca is one of the most emblematic Bolivian poets of her generation. But there is more than Elvira Espejo Ayca's poetry: she is also a visual artist, a storyteller, a singer, a weaver, a philosopher, a museum director, a teacher, a lecturer, and finally, she is also a binational Aymara-Quechua woman from the *Ayllu of Qaqachaka*, in the southern *Oruro* province, in the Central Andes – embracing millenary ancestral tradition, and making contemporary Bolivian culture shine internationally. For her outstanding commitment and engagement in culture in 2020 she was invested with the *Goethe Medaille*, the most prestigious distinction in culture awarded by the Federal Republic of Germany; in 2024 she was nominated *Chevalier des Arts et des Lettres* by the French Ministry of Culture; she has shown her art and represented Bolivia at some of the most prestigious international venues, such as the Venice Biennale, the Mercosul Biennale in Porto Alegre, the Museo Reina Sofía in Madrid and the House of World Cultures HKW Berlin; she won many prizes at Latin American poetry and literature festivals, in Bolivia, in Chile, in Cuba, in Venezuela; she held keynote addresses at international conferences and academic symposiums such as the CIMAM Annual Conference in Buenos Aires and the Instituto de Investigaciones Estéticas at UNAM in Mexico City; and last but not least, for almost twelve years now she has been directing the National Museum of Ethnography and Folklore (MUSEF) in La Paz, where she has not only established the museum as the most impressive contemporary site of cultural and knowledge production – publishing over 40 books, including eleven collection catalogues with over 500 pages each, conference readers, audio-visual documentaries and an educational animation series that has been widely critically acclaimed and broadcasted on international TV channels – after entirely redesigning the museography she has also made the MUSEF become the most visited museum in Bolivia for several years in a row.

Why insist in mentioning the many paths that Elvira Espejo Ayca's assiduous yet serene creative spirit has explored? Not because we would need to give proof of the fact that she is brilliant beyond what the reader will be able to find in this very book. Rather we think it is the other way round: we believe it is crucial to understand that Elvira's poetry stems from diverse origins and materialities, rooted in manifold artistic experiences and genealogies that unfold in the most diverse registers which are – condensed in a poem for example – inseparable one from the other.

In her work the song is inseparable from the poem, the poem inseparable from the grammar of weaving, the weaving inseparable from the oral tradition and Andean ancestrality, the ancestrality inseparable from the contemporary claim to decolonize Aymara and Quechua territory. *KIRKI QHAÑI* is in itself a bag of diverging moments and temporalities, a collection of innumerable voices, a container of Andean poetics.

This is crucial, because the multiplicity of Elvira's art doesn't seem to fit the minimizing stereotypes or trivializing categories that the globalized catalogs of cultural consumption seem to instantly hold ready for her. Ultimately, Elvira Espejo Ayca sings about building houses, she is a fierce and articulated thinker who dares speak out where others keep silent, pushing forward a political project of decolonization, situating Aymara ancestrality at the very center of the modern metropolis, where it coexists, contrasts and nurtures the busy lives that constitute today's Plurinational State of Bolivia.

Elvira Espejo Ayca is emblematic for contemporary Bolivia, because she represents as few others the simultaneous artistic, epistemological and political revolution that came about with the Plurinational State of Bolivia, with the unprecedented alliance of social and indigenous movements, worker's unions, miners and workers of the land that overturned the persistent legacy of the colonial state, and that gave birth to a new Political Constitution in 2009 finally bestowing dignity upon those who never stopped singing their ancestral songs during centuries of arduous pursuit for justice. And because Elvira Espejo Ayca represents this deeply rooted process of change in an exemplary way, it is important to translate her work – the work she recollects, the collective work she reconstructs – into other languages, bring her voice to other continents, make comprehensible the insoluble tie that connects the unrelenting claim of decolonization with the gentle song of the wanderer, with the wind, or with the rhythm of the poet's breath.

The present first English translation of *KIRKI QHAÑI / Petaca De Las Poéticas Andinas* only three years after its original Spanish-Aymara publication shows the pressing nature of this bundle of ancestral voices, of this poetic synthesis of the historical moment, to come to light along other lines of latitude, to reach new audiences, to pursue new alliances and to meet other urgencies.

Miami, Florida, 2025

INTRODUCCIÓN
ELVIRA ESPEJO AYCA DE NUESTROS ALIENTOS

Miguel Rocha Vivas
Universidad Javeriana, Bogotá, Cundinamarca, 2021

Conocí a Elvira Espejo Ayca mientras ella cantaba con una inolvidable voz aguda, la voz desnuda de un cántaro muy antiguo cuyas ondas de agua circulares son tan solo el reflejo, tan solo el espejo, de mundos más profundos contemporáneos a los nuestros. La belleza del arte verbal aymara expresa una sensibilidad de cuño colectivo cuya poética no sólo es un arte de la lengua, por sí sola, sino el tejido amplio de un lenguaje estructurado con funciones muy concretas: construir las casas, orientar la vida pastoril, aconsejar en la cotidianidad y sobre todo insuflar los alientos: *sami sami*.

Vivimos en una época en donde nos falta el aire. Esmog, virus y depresión son tan sólo síntomas de un desaliento que tiende a permearlo todo. Los alientos, *sami sami*, son cantos y ánimos que emergen de una relación armónica, aunque no idílica, con los cerros, los vientos y el conjunto bio-espiritual de la madre tierra. El lector de *Kirki Qhañi* /

INTRODUCTION
ELVIRA ESPEJO AYCA OF OUR BREATHS

Miguel Rocha Vivas
Javeriana University, Bogotá, Cundinamarca, 2021

I met Elvira Espejo Ayca while she sang with an unforgettable high-pitched voice, the naked voice of a very ancient jug whose circular water waves are only the reflection, just the mirror, of deeper worlds that are contemporary to ours. The beauty of Aymara's verbal art expresses a collective sensibility whose poetics is not only an art of language, by itself, but the broad fabric of a structured language with very specific functions: building houses, guiding pastoral life, advising in everyday life and above all insufflate the winds: *sami sami.*[1]

We live in a period in which we lack air. Smog, virus, and depression are just symptoms of an airlessness which tends to permeate everything. These breaths, *sami sami*, are songs

1 *Sami*. The word has multiple interwoven meanings referring to life essence such as color, luck, destiny, and breath. Color, breath, life (because through breathing life is possible), and air: the air that fills the lungs to live. Forces of life, sami also refers to the door to the state of life.

Petaca de las poéticas andinas, recibe un regalo de alientos a la vez que de palabras mayores, palabras sapienciales que forman parte de contextos culturales traducidos con sencillez y generosidad por Elvira Espejo Ayca.

La palabra de la abuela, su palabra más intima, es la que esta artista e investigadora tradicional aymara comienza por compartirnos. En las historias y cantos se vislumbra el calendario ceremonial andino que marca los ciclos de la tierra y de las comunidades que se derivan de ella. Las poéticas de la memoria, comenzando por la de la abuela Gregoria Mamani Sirqi, están contenidas en la imagen de la petaca. Desde su interior Espejo Ayca nos comparte poéticas rituales como las de pastoras y pastores que arreaban las piedras, los actos fundacionales del Inca, la peregrinación a los cerros, los alientos de la reproducción para los camélidos, en suma, *un camino infinito puluy puluy puluy puluy*.

El *sami* o aliento de la *minka* respira en *Kirki Qhañi*. La *pacha* o pluriverso hace brillar el pensamiento y las labores a modo de *minka*: reciprocidad, solidaridad, intercambio.

Jumas naya layku
Nayasay jumas layku
Mapitay irpasiñani
Sami sami sami

Ustedes por mi
Y yo por ustedes
Nos sobrellevaremos
Alientos, alientos, alientos

and spirits that emerge from a harmonious, although not idyllic, relationship with the hills, the winds, and the bio-spiritual unity with Mother Earth. The reader of *Kirki Qhañi / Container of Andean Poetics,*[2] receives a gift of blown encouragement at the same time as greater words, words of wisdom that are part of cultural contexts translated with simplicity and generosity by Elvira Espejo Ayca.

The word of the Grandmother, her most intimate word, is the word that this traditional Aymara artist and researcher begins by sharing with us. In the stories and songs, we discern the Andean ceremonial calendar that marks the cycles of the earth and the communities that come from it. Memetic poetics, beginning with the memories of Grandmother Gregoria Mamani Sirqi, are contained in the image of the container. From its interior, Espejo Ayca shares with us poetic rituals such as those of shepherds who carried stones, the founding actions of the Inca, the pilgrimage to the hills, the breaths of reproduction for the camelids, in summary, *an infinite path puluy puluy puluy puluy.*[3]

2 *Qhañi*. Refers to a container for textiles, a pouch, a portable sewing bag that also contains verses. It is a metaphor for a song that contains verses with information, as a mnemonic tool.

3 *Puluy*. Implies multiple meanings including the umbilical cord, human and textile, belly, abdomen, and bowels. Also, a round instrument. It is an instrument made from a hollowed-out gourd. The name *puluy puluy puluy* imitates the sound of this instrument linguistically. It is also the belly button, the breath that creates life, further representing femininity.

La voz del intenso trabajo colectivo que ha hecho célebres a la mujer y el hombre de los Andes, también llama a dar cuatro vueltas por el lugar de los descansos: *Sirkuy Sirkuy*. Se trata de una voz sapiencial que los lectores están llamados a resignificar sin desconocer los valores culturales intrínsecos del mundo aymara. El aliento *sami* se ofrece entonces como un equilibrio dinámico entre lo activo y lo pasivo, entre el hacer y el descansar adecuadamente, un conocimiento básico olvidado hoy debido al incesante fragor de una modernidad desconectada y sobrepuesta a los ciclos de la tierra.

La ancestralidad de *Kirki Qhañi* es futural, actual y contextual a la vez que reconoce pérdidas de cantos y ritualidades que procura restablecer a través de su recuento. La futuralidad de la poética ética y estética de Elvira Espejo es, como la de las actuales oralituras, una forma de resignificar los tejidos sociales sin perder los hilos, ni alterar las matrices básicas.

Elvira Espejo Ayca es una traductora entre culturas capaz de hacernos ver, pensar y sobre todo sentir. El carácter multimedial de su obra nunca se completa en sí mismo, siempre es un llamado a lo colectivo a la vez que un llamado a escuchar, texturar, entretejer miradas. Su obra de *sami* colectivo es una propuesta sentipensante en donde la oralidad, la escritura literaria alfabética y las grafías comunitarias, como el tejido, se combinan y confluyen en lo que he llamado oralitegrafías para referirme a la producción multimodal de algunos escritores indígenas actuales.

Kirki Qhañi es un llamado a la construcción de casas y lugares desde donde podamos conversar y converger preservando nuestras diferencias aunque con horizontes

The *sami* or breath of the *minka*[4] breathes in *Kirki Qhañi*. The *pacha* or pluriverse makes thought and labor shine like a *minka*: reciprocity, solidarity, exchange.

Jumas naya layku
Nayasay jumas layku
Mapitay irpasiñani
Sami sami sami

You for me
And I for you
We will cope
Breaths, breaths, breaths

The voice of the intense collective work that has made known the women and men of the Andes, also calls to wonder around the place of rests: *Sirkuy Sirkuy.*[5] It is about a wise voice that readers are called to redefine without ignoring the intrinsic cultural values of the Aymara world. The *sami* breath is then offered as a dynamic equilibrium between the active and the passive, between working and resting properly, a basic knowledge forgotten today due to the incessant roar of a modernity disconnected from and superimposed on the cycles of the earth.

4 *Minka*. An Andean tradition of community work that is carried out to help everyone. The word *minka* comes from the Quechua *minccacuni*, which means "to ask for help by promising something." It is a practice that seeks to synthesize relationships of reciprocity. In the *minka* community members come together to work on a common goal, such as building a house or harvesting a harvest.

5 *Sirkuy*. A resting place for those who are alive or those who are resting after death.

en común. Así como el ave *chiru chiru*, a quien se insta a construir en la parte más alta del barranco, desde donde pueda tener una visión de conjunto para protegerse de los depredadores, aquellos incapaces de construir paredes de adobes de azúcar, de recibir los cantos de las abuelas, crear con piedras pesadas, o hilos livianos, y respetar el baile de *chinchilla*.

Las poéticas rituales de *Kirki Qhañi*, petaca que contiene agua limpia de las acequias y de los ríos profundos del cielo y de la tierra, son frutos de un cultivo ancestral y futuro, un aporte sensible al tejido complejo de nuestros mundos, para *estar siempre creciendo como el árbol del molle:*

Plantada y plantada *está muy bien plantada.*

The ancestry of *Kirki Qhañi* is of the future, the present and contextual while recognizing losses of songs and rituals that it attempts to restore through its recounting. The future of Elvira Espejo Ayca's ethical and aesthetic poetics is, like that of current ancestral oral traditions, a way of redefining social fabrics without losing the threads or altering the basic matrices.

Elvira Espejo Ayca is a translator between cultures capable of making us see, think and above all feel. The multimedia character of her work is never complete in itself, it is always a call to the collective as well as a call to listen, to give texture, interweave glances. Her collective *sami* work is a thoughtful proposal of feeling and thought where orality, alphabetic literary writing, and community handwriting, such as weaving, combine and converge in what I have called oralitegraphies to refer to the multimodal production of some current indigenous writers.

Kirki Qhañi is a call to build houses and places from where we can talk and converge preserving our differences but with common horizons. Like the *chiru chiru* bird, that has the need to build in the highest part of the ravine, from where it can have a collective overview to protect itself from predators, to those incapable of building adobe sugar walls, of receiving the songs of grandmothers, of creating with heavy stones, or light threads, and respecting the *chinchilla*[6] dance.

6 *Chinchilla*. A small mammal native to the Andes, also meaning a very fine and brilliant coat. The silk of the Andes.

The poetic rituals of *Kirki Qhañi*, a container that contains clean water from irrigation canals and the deep rivers of the sky and the earth, are the fruits of ancestral and future crops, a sensitive contribution to the complex fabric of our worlds, *to be always growing like the molle tree*:

Planted and planted *it is very well planted.*

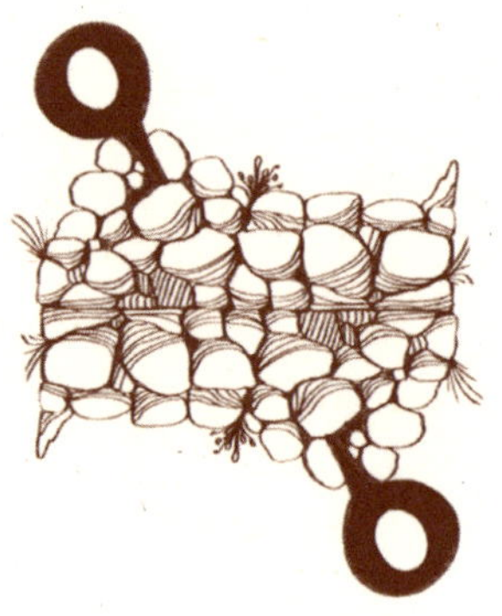

SAMI KIRKI

SONG TO THE SACRED BREATHS

Gregoria Mamani cuenta de su abuela Martina Pumala. En aquellos tiempos, mi abuela Gregoria Mamani (1900) escuchó la memoria de su abuela doña Martina Pumala (1700), quien le reveló que los cantos tenían tanta fuerza que podrían responder al universo, por ejemplo el canto al sol en el mes de junio, el canto a las nubes en el mes de octubre, o el canto a la nueva producción en el mes de febrero, todos con una dinámica distinta.

El canto a Pucara, según mi abuela, fue uno de los más importantes de la región, era como un agradecimiento con todo el aliento al gran guardián de la comunidad; para este canto todo el pueblo se preparaba para subir al cerro cantando. Según la narración de mi abuela, las autoridades organizaban esta ceremonia comunal, en la que las mujeres llevaban veleros *micha chuwas* en la mano y los varones llevaban una cerámica con fuego *niña k'ara*, el fuego envuelto en cenizas para que no se apagara y una fuente de cerámica grande *jach'a phuntilla* para el ritual. Los niños y las niñas llevaban agua en cántaros *yuru* y algunas hojas verdes y flores sagradas del lugar, y subían al cerro cantando.

Al llegar al cerro todos trabajaban en la preparación de la ceremonia. Llenaban la fuente de cerámica grande *jach'a phuntilla* con agua llevada por los niños y niñas, donde depositaban los pétalos de las flores sagradas, *tani tani* de las alturas, *chana chana* de la parte media, *putu putu* de los valles y las hojas de coca verde. En medio de esta fuente de agua las mujeres depositaron la *micha chuwa*, con grasa de llama *untu* prendida. Por otro lado, las autoridades preparaban el fuego para hacer la ofrenda al cerro guardián de las almas del pueblo, pidiendo permiso al agua, al fuego, al viento y al cerro guardián del territorio. La poética se centra en el cerro

Gregoria Mamani speaks of her grandmother Martina Pumala. In those times, my grandmother Gregoria Mamani (1900) listened to the memory of her grandmother Doña Martina Pumala (1700), who revealed to her that the songs were so powerful that they could respond to the universe: for example the song of the June sun, the song of the October clouds, or the song of the new production in the month of February, each with a distinct dynamic.

The song to Pukara, according to my grandmother, was one of the most important in the region, it was like a thank you with all the breath, a thank you to the great guardian of the community. For this song the entire town made preparations to climb the hill singing. According to my grandmother's story, the authorities organized this communal ceremony, in which the women carried *micha chuwas*[7] candle holders in their hands and the men carried a pottery with *niña k'ara*[8] fire – wrapped in ashes so that the fire will not go out – and a large ceramic *jach'a phuntilla* fountain for the ritual. The boys and girls carried water in *yuru*[9] jugs and green leaves and flowers from the sacred place and climbed the hill singing.

Arriving at the hill, everyone worked in preparation for the ceremony. They filled the large, ceramic *jach'a phuntilla*

7 *Chuwas*. A small clay dish in which you put a candle to shine, giving light.

8 *Niña k'ara.* A bird with fire sparks. According to the stories it is a nocturnal bird. A secondary meaning is a person transporting fire in a clay vessel.

9 *Yuru*. A medium sized jug used normally to carry liquids such as water or ceremonial drinks such as *Chicha*. It is used in offerings.

sagrado, actualmente *uywiri* en la lengua aymara, el criador de la vida. Luego pasarán al ciclo de las nubes, como cantar a las neblinas, a las nubes, a la lluvia, a la apertura de la tierra, a las semillas, al color de las estrellas, al brillo de la luna, al viento y a todos los seres del universo, a los *sami*, alientos que acompañan a unos y otros a lo largo de la vida. Las poéticas también nos narran los distintos periodos de la memoria, como el lenguaje de *tupuraya* en lengua pukina, en lengua quechua pukara de los incas, y finalmente *uywiri* en la actualidad aymara, precisando al mismo lugar del cerro como el gran guardián de la región. Esta nos permite entender que en la zona tuvieron tres periodos distintos en los cantos poéticos, que se cultivaron en la memoria oral del pueblo mencionado, poéticas que nos llevan a distintos tiempos de la vida sagrada. Todos estos cantos de las ceremonias ancestrales eran practicados antes de la historia colonial y durante la colonia se fusionaron con los cantos católicos, dando como resultado un amalgama entre lo que el pueblo comprende y la iglesia obliga. No obstante, esta práctica crecerá paulatinamente hasta que los cantos católicos se apoderen completamente del lenguaje, de aquellos cantos sagrados heredados del pueblo incario, dejando solamente los cantos religiosos católicos que se cantan en las iglesias católicas.

Así cuenta mi abuela de aquellos tiempos y aquellos cantos que hoy han desaparecido.

En memoria de mi querida abuela Gregoria Mamani Sirqi.

fountain with the water carried by the boys and girls where they deposited the petals of the sacred *tani tani*[10] flowers from the heights, *chana chana*[11] from the middle part, *putu putu*[12] from the valleys and the leaves of green coca. In the middle of this fountain, the women placed the *micha chuwa*, with llama fat *untu,*[13] which has been lit. On the other side, the authorities prepared the fire for the offering to the guardian hill for the souls of the town, asking permission from the water, the fire, the wind and the guardian hill of the territory. The poetics focuses on the sacred hill, known as *uywiri*[14] in the Aymara language, the creator of life. Later, they will move on to the cloud cycle, how to sing to the mists, to the clouds, to the rain, to the opening of the earth, to the seeds, to the color of the stars, to the brightness of the moon, to the wind and to all the beings of the universe, to the *sami* – breaths that accompany each other throughout life. The poetics also tell us about the different periods of memory, such as the language of

10 *Tani tani*. Are sacred flowers used in ceremonies, grown in high, middle, and low elevations.

11 *Chana chana*. A sacred flower from the valley used in carnival.

12 *Putu putu*. A sacred red flower from the valley only used for special offerings.

13 *Untu*. Fat or suet, usually from llama, used as an offering or as medicine.

14 *Uywiri*. A mountain deity, sacred hill, guardian, protector and creator. It translates directly as nurturer, or the one who nurtures. It is also referred to as a place that protects its inhabitants.

tupuraya[15] in the Pukina language, in the Quechua Pukara language of the Incas, and finally *uywiri* in present-day Aymara, specifying the same place on the hill as the great guardian of the region. This enables us to understand that they had three distinct periods of poetic songs in the region, cultivated in the oral memory of the aforementioned people, poetics that take us to different times of sacred life. All these songs from ancestral ceremonies were practiced before the colonial period, and during colonial times they merged with Catholic songs, resulting in an amalgamation between what the people understand and what the church obliges. This practice will gradually grow until Catholic songs completely take over the language, those sacred songs inherited from the Incan people, leaving only the Catholic religious songs that are sung in Catholic churches.

This is how my grandmother tells of those times and those songs that have disappeared today.

In memory of my dear grandmother Gregoria Mamani Sirqi.

15 *Tupuraya* is *pukara*, or uywiri, a sacred, protective hill: a place that protects its inhabitants, from the Pukina language.

Pukar sami[16] — Breath of Pukara[17]

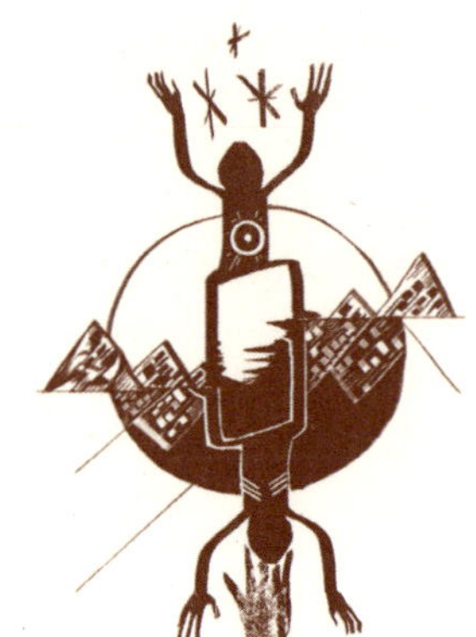

Intitalay jalantjipana
Tupurayar sarañani

Ititalay jalantjipana
Pukararuy sarañani

Wara waray willinuqthipana
Tupurayar irsuñani

Wara waray willinuqthipana
Pukararuy irsuñani

Kuna laykuy irsuñani
Sami laykuy irsuñani

Kuna laykuy irsuñani
Uwir laykuy irsuñani

16 *Sami*. Breath, life, air.

17 *Pukara*. A protective deity. A sacred hill, guardian, protector and creator. A place that protects its inhabitants.

When the sun sets
We go together to Tupuraya[18]

When the sun sets
We go to Pukara

When the stars are spilled across the sky
We will reach Tupuraya

When the stars are spilled across the sky
We will reach Pukara

To what will we rise together?
We will rise by our breaths

To what will we rise together?
We will rise for our guide

18 *Tupuraya*. Sacred, protective hill.

Phaxsi sami
– Breath of the Moon

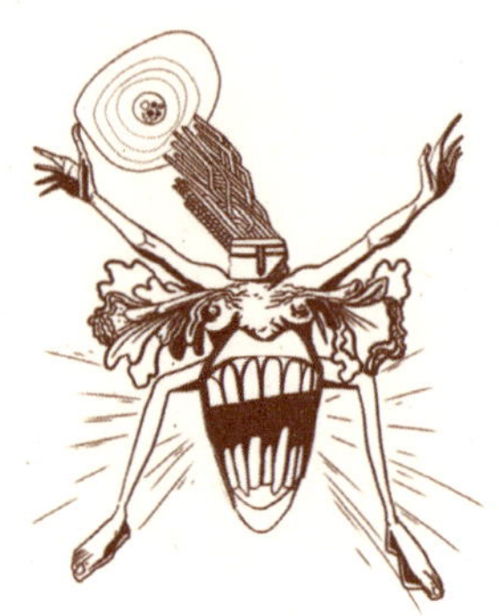

Phaxsi sami qhana qhana qhana qhanay
Amtayarachh sami qhana qhana qhanay

Muspamaya sami qhana qhana qhana qhanay
Phaxsi qhana sami qhana qhana qhanay

Warmi qhana sami qhana qhana qhana qhanay
Mira kasta sami qhana qhana qhanay

Kinsa ch´íwu sami qhana qhana qhana qhanay
Pusi ch´iwu sami qhana qhana qhanay

Muyupaya sami qhana qhana qhana qhanay
Mira kasta sami qhana qhana qhanay

Breaths of the moon shine, shine, shine, shine
Breaths of knowledge shine, shine, shine

Breaths of a dream shine, shine, shine, shine
Breaths of the breathing moon shine, shine, shine

White breaths of a woman shine, shine, shine, shine
Breaths of a flowering shine, shine, shine

Breaths of three shadows shine, shine, shine, shine
Breaths of four shadows shine, shine, shine

Breaths that revolve around me shine, shine, shine, shine
Breaths of reproduction shine, shine, shine

Wara wara sami
— Breath of the Stars

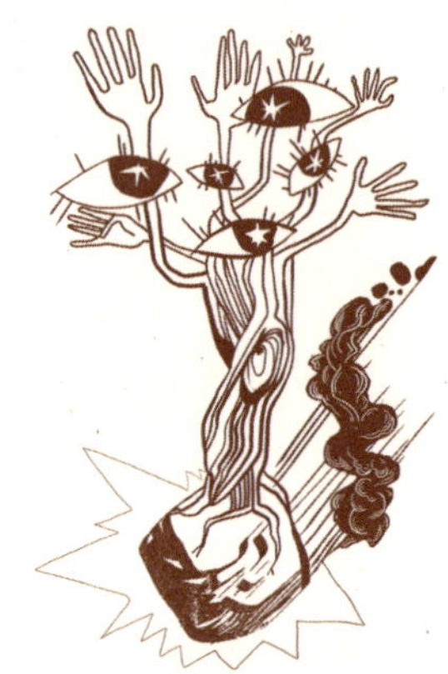

Wara waray aywinuqjipanay
Pukaratway arurapima
Lliphi lliphi chuyma katukama
Lliphi lliphi lluqu katukama

Wara waray lliphipjipanay
Uywiritway arurapima
Lliphi lliphi wila katukama
Lliphi lliphi sinta katukama

Wara waray qutuchasjipanay
Maya chuymay arurapima
Lliphi lliphi amuyt´ayapxita
Lliphi lliphi irpasiwayapxita

When the stars arrive
From Pukara[19] I will greet you
The lightening that sustains the lung
The lightening that sustains the heart

When the stars shine
From my great protector I will greet you
The brightness that sustains the blood
The shine that sustains the path

When the stars come together
From my heart I will greet you
The shine that makes us think
The shine that guides us

19 *Pukara*. A protective deity. A sacred hill, guardian, protector, and creator.

Ch´iwu sami
– Breath of the Clouds

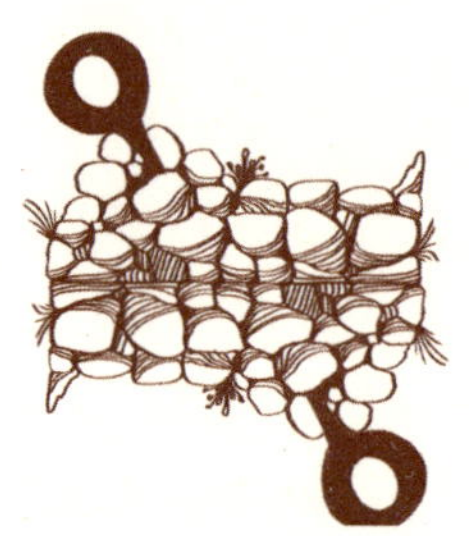

Janq´ u urpu sami
patxaranar sami

Chiyar urpu sami
manqharanar sami

Wila urpu sami
chuyma manqhar sami

Janq´u chiwu sami
wayra muyu sami

Chiyar ch´iwu sami
jallu ch´iwu sami

Wila ch´iwu sami
llaki ch´iwu sami

Breath of a white mist
That breathes upward

Breath of a black mist
That breathes downwards

Breath of a red mist
Who breathes from the bottom of the lung

Breath of white clouds
Who breathe towards the wind that turns

Breath of a black cloud
That breathes from the rain

Breath of a red cloud
That breathes towards sadness

Puluy puluy – The Circle of a Puluy[20]

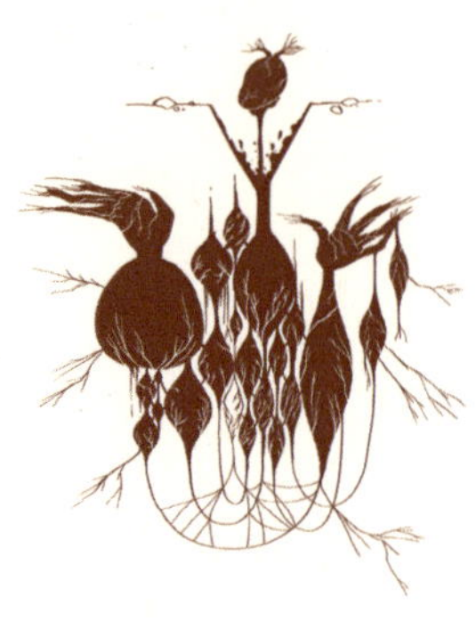

Sami miray puluy puluy puluy puluy
Amta yarachh maya puluy puluy puluy

Wila lamar punku puluy puluy puluy puluy
Sami lliph punku puluy puluy puluy

Wila lluqu sami puluy puluy puluy puluy
Kasta sami puluy puluy puluy

Mira kasta sami puluy puluy puluy puluy
Sinta maya sami puluy puluy puluy

20 *Puluy*. Umbilical cord, belly, belly button, abdomen, and bowels. An instrument made from a hollowed-out gourd.

Spirits of reproduction puluy puluy puluy puluy
Full of knowledge puluy puluy puluy puluy

The red sea gate puluy puluy puluy puluy
The door that shines with breath puluy puluy puluy puluy

The breath of a red heart puluy puluy puluy puluy
All kinds of breaths puluy puluy puluy puluy

In which is reproduced puluy puluy puluy puluy
An infinite path puluy puluy puluy puluy

Sami sami — Breaths

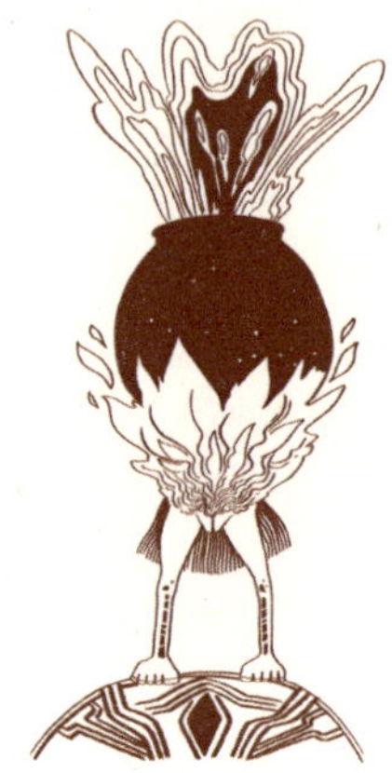

Inti sami
Phaxsi sami
Wara wara sami
Wayra sami
Uraq sami
Phaqar sami
Jumas naya layku
Nayasay jumas layku
Mapitay irpasiñani
Sami sami sami

Breath of the sun
Breath of the moon
Breath of the stars
Breath of the wind
Breath of the earth
Breath of the flowers
You for me
And I for you
We will carry each other
Breaths, breaths, breaths

Sama sirku
– The Place of Rests

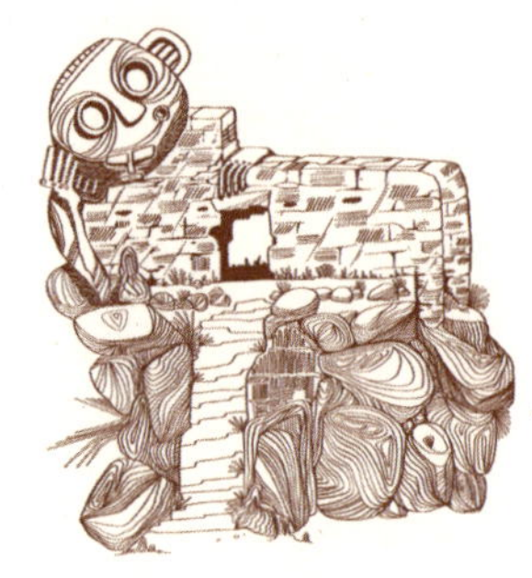

Sirkuy sirkuy sama sirkuy
Mayat muytanim sama sikuy

Sirkuy sirkuy jisk´a sirkuy
Payat muytanim sama sirkuy

Sirkuy sirkuy taypi sirkuy
kimsat muytanim sama sirkuy

Sirkuy sirkuy yach´á sirkuy
pusit muytanim sama sirkuy

Sirkuy sirkuy sama sirkuy
Walit muytanim sama sirkuy

Sirkuy sirkuy,[21] place of rests
Take a walk around the placc of rests

Sirkuy sirkuy, small sirkuy
Take a second lap around the place of rests

Sirkuy sirkuy, central sirkuy
Take the third lap around the place of rests

Sirkuy sirkuy, big sirkuy
Take the fourth lap around the place of rests

Sirkuy sirkuy, place of rests
Take a walk remembering the place of rests

21 *Sirkuy*. A resting place for those who are alive and those who are resting after death.

Simay maya[22]
– Only Once a Week

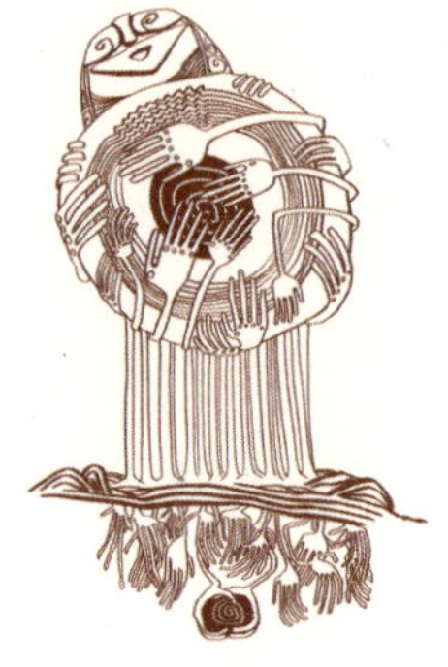

Alawatu sinsalsismu
Siman purismay simanchay
Siman may sinsalsismu
Alawatu sinsalsismu
Siman purismay simanchay
Siman may sinsalsismu
Jisus jisusay mari jusi way
Jisus jisusay mari jusi way

Alawatu sinsalsismu
Siman purismay simanchay
Siman may sinsalsismu
Alawatu sinsalsismu
Siman purismay simanchay
Siman may sinsalsismu
Jisus jisusay mari jusi way
Jisus jisusay mari jusi way

22 *Simay maya*. Songs sung once per week.

Praised and exalted
If you would come for a week
You would be exalted for a week
Praised and exalted
If you would come for a week
You would be exalted for a week
Jesus, Jesus, Mary and Joseph
Jesus, Jesus, Mary and Joseph

Praised and exalted
If you came for a week
You would be exalted for a week
Praised and exalted
If you came for a week
You would be exalted for a week
Jesus, Jesus, Mary and Joseph
Jesus, Jesus, Mary and Joseph

Phanchay liryusa[23] — Blooming Lillies

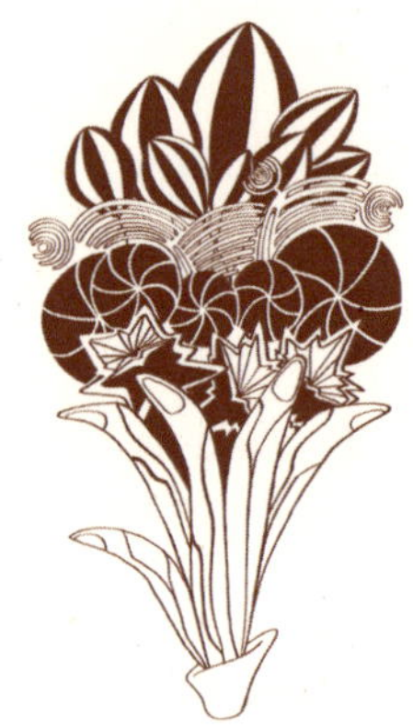

Phanchay liryusay
Tatitu sumay phaqhalay
Phanchay liryusay
Tatitu sumay phaqhalay
Paxaranay tani tani tatituy
Taypiranay chana chana tatituy
Manqaranay putu putu tatituy
Phanchay liryusay
Tatitu sumay phaqhalay
Phanchay liryusay
Tatitu sumay phaqhalay

23 *Phanchay liryusa*. Blooming lilies, symbolize opening one's heart, space, mind, and soul.

The lord of good flowers
It blooms like a lily
The lord of good flowers
It blooms like a lily
At the highest part it blooms like tani tani[24]
In the middle part it blooms like chana chana[25]
In the lowest part it blooms like putu putu[26]
The lord of good flowers
It blooms like a lily
The lord of good flowers
It blooms like a lily

24 *Tani Tani*. Sacred flowers used in ceremonies, grown in high, middle, and low elevations.

25 *Chana chana*. Sacred flower from the valley used in carnival.

26 *Putu putu*. Sacred red flower from the valley only used for special offerings. Like *putu putu* that is also used for special offerings and *chana chana* that is used in carnival: *putu putu* is likewise a sacred flower.

Aruray[27] arura — Greetings to the Sky

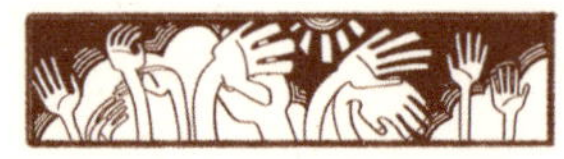

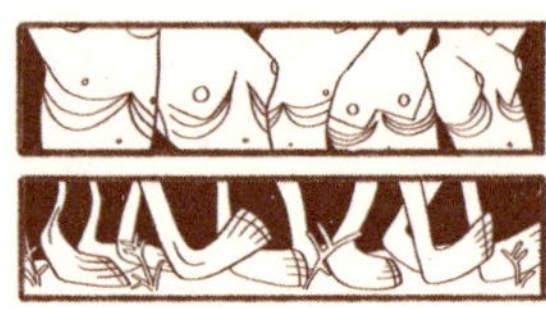

Aruray aruray
Siluy aruray
Tati sumay phaqhalay
Aruray aruray
Siluy aruray
Tati sumas phaqalay
Khistirakiy kamachistu tatituy
Tuluris mamitay kamachistu tatituy
Kamsasaray kamachistu tatituy
Istachhun saram san kamachistu tatituy
Istachhun saram san kamachistu tatituy
Jina jianay istachhuna tatituy
Jina jinay istachhuna tatituy
Khistirakiy kamachistu tatituy
Richhuristalay kamachistu tatituy

27 *Aruray*. To greet, to salute, and to communicate via a medium.

Greetings, greetings
To the intense sky
To the lord of good flowers
Greetings, greetings
To the intense sky
To the lord of good flowers
Who has guided us, Lord?
La señora Dolores[28] has guided us, Lord
Why has she guided us, Lord?
So that we go in procession, Lord
So that we go in procession, Lord
Come on, let's go in procession, Lord
Come on, let's go in procession, Lord
Who has guided us, Lord?
The Lord of prayers, Lord

28 *Señora Dolores*. Partially a Catholic appropriation, this concept developed to symbolize the integration of the Catholic and the Aymara community. The Virgin Mary transforms into Pachamama, or Mother earth, sick from the exploitation of the land in Potosí.

Salwi salwi[29] — Salwi Salwi

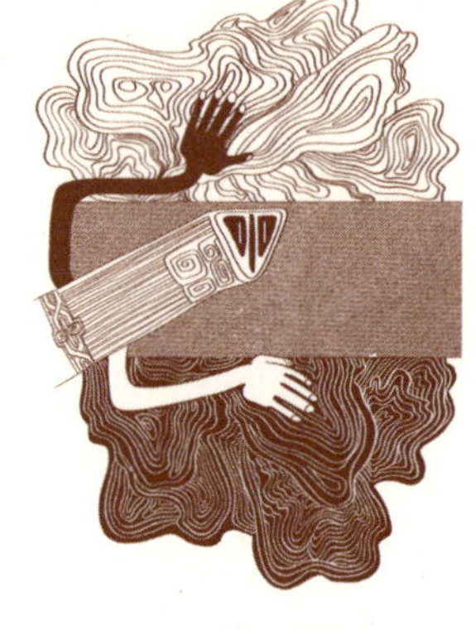

Salwi salwi yusti salwi
Mari miryuy micercordiyay
Mari miryuy micercordiyay
Kuna juchan juchachata yusti salwi
Ch´aphi juchan juchachata yusti salwi

Salwi salwi justi salwi
María miryuy micercordiyay
María miryuy micercordiyay
Kuna k´anchan k´anchayata yusti salwi
Qhispi K´anchan k´anchayata yusti salwi

Salwi salwi justi salwi
Mari miryuy micercordiyay
Mari miryuy micercordiyay
Kuna kayun makatita yusti salwi
Qunqur kayun makatita yusti salwi

Salwi salwi justi salwi
María miryuy misercordiyay
María miryuy misercordiyay
Kuna irpan irpata yusti salwi
Urpu irpan irpata yusti salwi.
Salwi salwi justi salwi
María miryuy misercordiyay
María miryuy misercordiyay

29 *Salwi*. A joining of the Catholic concept of salvation with the Aymara traditional herb of healing.

Hail, hail, may God save you
Mary of mercy
Mary of mercy
Why does God save you?
Because of the thorns God save you

Hail, hail, may God save you
Mary of mercy
Mary of mercy
With what luminosity has it illuminated you? God save you
With the luminosity of quispi[30] he has illuminated me, God save you

Hail, hail, may God save you
Mary of mercy
Mary of mercy
With what walk have you walked? God save you
With the walking of my knees I have walked, God save you

Hail, hail, may God save you
Mary of mercy
Mary of mercy
With what walk have you walked? God save you
The path of mist, God save you
Hail, hail, may God save you
Mary of mercy
Mary of mercy

30 *Quispi*. To illuminate the life of someone or something, awakening the spirit or the soul.

Paskusis urusisa[31] — For Easter

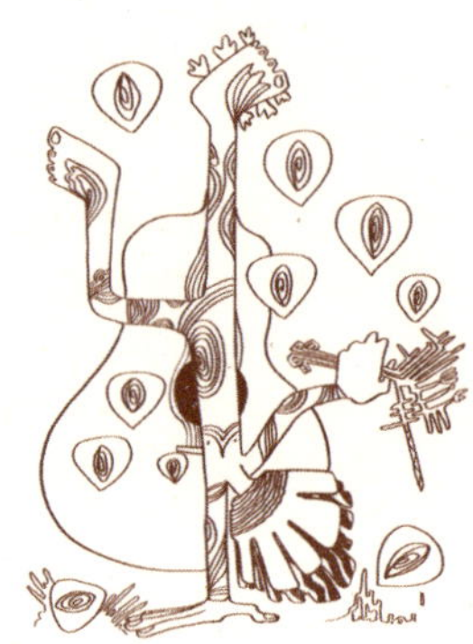

Paskusisay urusiay paskusay
Jumana naya uruñankay
Phaqharas laya piñay paskusay

Paskusisay urusiay paskusay
Jumana naya uruñankay
Rusas t'ikhapiñay paskusay

Paskusisay urusiay paskusay
Jumana naya uruñankay
Phaqaras pasmjipiña paskusay

Paskusisay urusiay paskusay
Lakas chixchipacha iñarpayanista paskusay

Paskusisay urusiay paskusay
Layras titi pacha iñarpayanista paskusay

31 *Urusisa*. A full day of celebration, a day of festivity, the best day of celebration, where the community gathers, talks, and enjoys the abundance of the new harvest. Uru is Quechua, sisa is Aymara, so the word itself is a joining of Quechua and Aymara with the Catholic day of Easter.

Celebrating the urusisa Easter Day
In your day and in my day
The flowers are of every color

Celebrating urusisa Easter Day
In your day and in my day
Even the roses are in full bloom

Celebrating urusisa Easter Day
In your day and in my day
Even the flowers wither

Celebrating urusisa Easter Day
With an immense smile you look at me, Easter

Celebrating urusisa Easter Day
With intense eyes you look at me, Easter

Paskusisay urusiay paskusay
Luxhu kitarmantis luxhurpayanitay paskusay

Paskusisay urusiay paskusay
Q´ara turasnuntis jaqurpayanjitay paskusay

Jumana urumankay tirijus parwayuway paskusay
Nayanuruñankas tunqusa parwayuway paskusay

Jumana urumankay timpus mayapiñay paskusay
Nayana uruñankay phaqharas pasmjipiña paskusay

Celebrating urusisa Easter Day
With guitar chords you welcomed me, Easter

Celebrating urusisa Easter Day
At least throw me the peaches of the season, Easter

On your day, even the ears of barley bloom, Easter
On my day, even the ears of corn bloom, Easter

In your day there is only one time, Easter
In my time even the flowers wither, Easter

Kunaraki jan jachi — What Doesn't Cry?

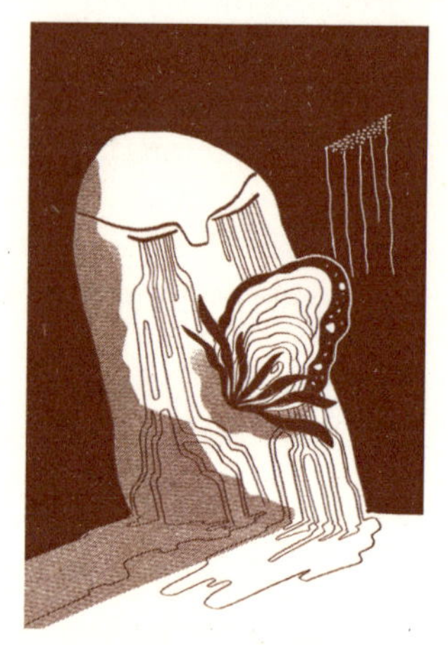

Wayra mayas jachi
Phaxcha umas jachi
Jachan jachan ruyrusitu
Jachan jachan ruyrusitu

Kunaraki jan jachaspa
Kawkiraki jan jachaspa
Jachan jachan ruyrusitu
Jachan jachan ruyrusitu

Jamch'isay jachi
Chuyma mayas jachi
Jachan jachan ruyrusitu
Jachan jachan ruyrusitu

Qala mayas jachi
Sumat qhanat warari
Jachan jachan ruyrusitu
Jachan jachan ruyrusitu

Uywa mayas janchi
Liq'umayas jachi
Jachan jachan ruyrusitu
Jachan jachan ruyrusitu

Quqa mayas jachi
Alimayas jachi
Jachan jachan ruyrusitu
Jachan jachan ruyrusitu

Even the wind cries
Even the waterfalls cry
I only cry inside
I only cry inside

Who doesn't cry?
What doesn't cry?
I only cry inside
I only cry inside

Even the birds cry
From the bottom of their hearts, they cry
I only cry inside
I only cry inside

Even the stones cry
In front and secretly, they cry
I only cry inside
I only cry inside

Even animals cry
Even the bugs cry
I only cry inside
I only cry inside

Even the trees cry
Even the bushes cry
I only cry inside
I only cry inside

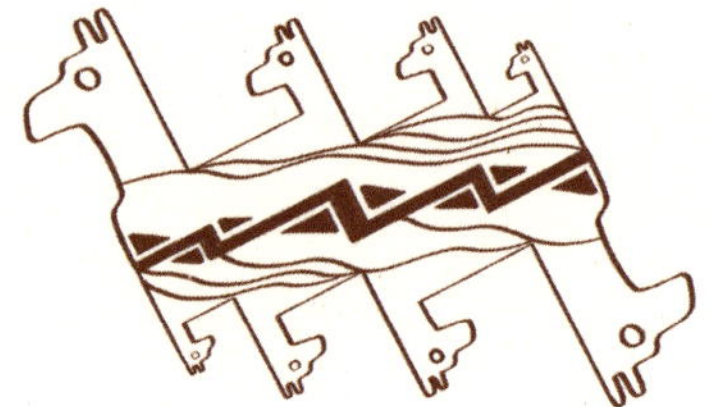

THAKHI — LA SENDA

THAKHI — THE PATH

Las pastoras y los pastores de la región de Qaqachaka cuentan que la crianza mutua del rebaño, *uywaña*, fue en torno al ciclo pastoril de la vida del rebaño.

Para tener los mejores camélidos uno tenía que arrear desde las montañas más altas, en especial las crías envueltas en *awayu* o rebozos para mantenerlos en calor. Para el cuidado de las crías, para su mejor crianza, todo el pueblo se dedicaba a recolectar los mejores pastos para su alimentación y las mejores semillas para su diseminación y crecimiento de los pastizales. Desde los ojos de agua, *uma phuju*, se las conducía al almacenador de agua, *uma pirwa o uma putu*, desde allá se las llevaba en canales de agua, *uma larq'a*, para la distribución del agua en todos los espacios posibles donde crecían los mejores pastos para atraer a todos los animales y tener los más grandes y mejores rebaños del altiplano, donde comenzó la crianza mutua. El cuidado de las hembras será primordial para el pueblo, por la vulnerabilidad de las crías. Los machos serán separados y llevados a otros espacios lejos de las hembras. Esta rutina del ciclo de la crianza de camélidos genera una serie de ritualidades poéticas: desde el dominio de los espacios, como los paisajes de cerros, pampas, ríos y ojos de aguas, hasta la llegada de las crías como una nueva generación, en la que nace la poética de su llegada a la familia (las crías recibirán los nuevos aretes *qarwa phaqhara* y collares *walqha* para su identificación de género y la correspondencia a la familia que pertenecerá). Estas ritualidades se centran en el mes de diciembre, *machaq qallun urupa*, día de la nueva generación. Familias enteras cantan a la integración mutua de vidas. Después de dos años con el rebaño de las madres, los machos serán separados en el mes de febrero, *qarwa k'illpha*, para el marcado y la distribución del rebaño

The shepherds of the Qaqachaka region say that the mutual raising of the flock, *uywaña,*[32] revolved around the flock's pastoral cycle of life.

To have the best camelids one had to herd them from the highest mountains. To keep them warm, the young were specially wrapped in *awayu*[33] shawls. For the care of the young, to best raise them, the entire town dedicated themselves to collecting the best grasses for feed and to gather the best seeds for the dissemination and growth of the grasslands. From the *uma*[34] *phuju,*[35] or water holes, water was directed to storage, *uma pirwa*[36] or *uma putu,* and then distributed via irrigation canals called *uma larq'a,* to the range of possible spaces where the young were raised. The best pastures attracted the largest and best herds on the Altiplano, where shared tending of the herd began. The care of the female camelids was essential due to the vulnerability of the young. The male camelids were separated and taken to other spaces away from the females. This routine of the

32 *Uywaña.* To nurture or to rear mutually and let oneself be reared; to mutually educate and protect.

33 *Awayu.* A traditional hand-woven cloth from the Andes used to carry food, babies and other important things, it is also used as a cover blanket for comfort and warmth.

34 *Uma.* Water, the primordial liquid flowing in our bodies, in space, in the land, and in time.

35 *Phuju.* A crystal-clear spring or pool with magical powers of nourishment.

36 *Pirwa.* A large community storage place for the storage and distribution of resources such as food and textiles.

a la familia correspondiente. En esta ritualidad los machos jovencitos serán arreados a *urqu tama*, al territorio de machos *purta*, donde se integran con las otras generaciones, para conocer el domino del territorio y recibir una mejor alimentación. Los machos adultos eran arreados a la ceremonia ritual del cruce, *qarwa jarqhaya*, donde la poética se apoderaba de la voz femenina y masculina, para que los jóvenes y niños del pueblo aprendan del ciclo de la crianza mutua. Al tercer año de vida, el rebaño de machos jóvenes viajaba por primera vez a los valles, junto a sus pastores, llevando sal, lana, y yerbas de altura (como la *Chacha Cuma*) para el intercambio de mercadería y el consumo. En esta ritualidad de su partida a los valles, los jóvenes machos eran jerarquizados según su comportamiento: el *irpa irpa* o delantero, los tres machos recibirán *qarwa sinsiru*, como el gran líder, guiador y guardián de toda la tropa de viajeros. Al retornar de los valles al pueblo de las alturas eran recibidos con otra ceremonia de la buena llegada, con cantos poéticos de su trajín, de los territorios atravesados con valentía y acompañando a la familia. La poética se apodera de esas memorias por la llegada de una gran variedad de maíz, que será celebrada con recuerdo del camino y el intercambio de vidas, mientras el rebaño de viajeros será arreado a su territorio natal, purta, para seguir con el ciclo de la vida. Todas estas ritualidades poéticas nos acercan a la crianza mutua del rebaño sistemático, como memorias orales de la vida, en los que la poética cumple este rol de las vidas mutuas del entorno, sentimientos profundos convertidos en poética del pueblo, que se transmitirá de una generación a otra, como ciclos poéticos continuos de la vida.

camelid breeding cycle generates a series of poetic rituals: from the domain of spaces, such as the landscapes of hills, pampas, rivers and springs, to the arrival of the offspring as a new generation, in that the poetics of their arrival in the family is born. (The young will receive the new *qarwa phaqhara*[37] earrings and *walqha* necklaces for their gender identification and correspondence to the family to which they will belong). These rituals focus on the month of December, *machaq qallun urupa*, day of the new generation. Entire families sing of the mutual integration of lives. After two years with the mothers' herd, the males will be separated in the month of February, *qarwa k'illpha*, for marking and distribution of the herd to the corresponding family. In this ritual, the young males will be herded to *urqu tama,*[38] to the territory of *purta*[39] machos, where they integrate with the other generations, to learn the domain of the territory and receive a better alimentation. The adult males were herded to the ritual crossing ceremony, *qarwa jarqhaya*, where poetics took over the female and male voice, so that the youth and children of the village could learn from the cycle of mutual raising. In the third year of life, the herd of young males traveled for the first time to the valleys, together with their shepherds, carrying salt, wool, and high-altitude herbs (such

37 *Qarwa phaqhara*. Earrings for llamas. (Qarwa is llama and phaqhara is flower).

38 *Urqu tama*. Male herd. Urqu is the male llama, selected to guide the baby male llamas. Tama is the herd, also a numerous family moving in unity.

39 *Purta*. A place where only male llamas can live.

as *Chacha Cuma*[40]) for the exchange of merchandise and consumption. In this ritual of their departure to the valleys, the young machos were ranked according to their behavior: the *irpa irpa*[41] or leader, the three machos will receive *qarwa sinsiru,*[42] as the great leader, guide and guardian of the entire troop of travelers. Upon returning from the valleys to the town in the heights, they were received with another ceremony of good arrival, with poetic songs of their work, of the territories bravely crossed and accompanying the family. The poetic takes hold of these memories due to the arrival of a great variety of corn, which will be celebrated with remembrance of the journey and the exchange of lives, while the herd of travelers will be herded to their native territory, *purta*, to continue the cycle of life. All these poetic rituals bring us closer to the systematic, mutual raising of the flock, as oral memories of life, in which the poetic fulfills this role of the shared lives of the environment, deep feelings converted into poetics of the people, which will be transmitted from one generation to the next, as continuous poetic cycles of life.

40 *Chuca Cuma*. A fragrant and branchy plant that has been used by indigenous populations to treat altitude sickness, stomach pain and other ailments.

41 *Irpa*. The one who leads. Irpa Irpa is the one who guides the flocks through paths with bravery and valor in the best way possible.

42 *Qarwa sinsiru*. A bell that llamas wear on their collar, its ring symbolically opens new spaces and paths.

Chullumpi[43] — Grebe

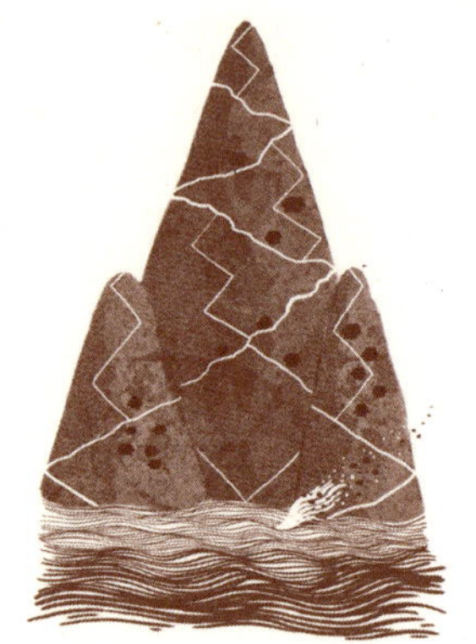

Kawkiy ukat antastha
Waya waya wayay chullumpi
Jila lumat antastha
Waya waya wayay chullumpi
Kawkiy ukat qushtastha
Waya waya wayay chullumpi
Turu maykut qushtastha
Waya waya wayay chullumpi
Kawkiy ukat jiktastha
Waya waya wayay chullumpi
Jujchu t´allat jiktastha
Waya waya wayay chullumpi
Kuna kamay antastha
Waya waya wayay chullumpi
Kumpiriskamay antastha
Waya waya wayay chullumpi

43 *Chullumpi*. Grebe. Waves in a lake formed made by the grebe. A mythological Andean bird that also poetically describes the waves that form in the long hair of the llama when the wind blows.

From where have you herded
The breeding path of the grebe
From the high hill I herd
The breeding path of the grebe
From where did you rise
The breeding path of the grebe
From turu mallku[44] I herded them
The breeding path of the grebe
From where did I raise it
The breeding path of the grebe
From jujchu t'alla[45] I brought them
The breeding path of the grebe
What color did I herd them
The breeding path of the grebe
In candied-colors I herded them
The breeding path of the grebe

44 *Turu mallku*. A sacred male protector hill that cares for the inhabitants of the area.

45 *Jujchu t'alla*. A sacred female protector hill that cares for the inhabitants of the area.

Wawachastha saktha[46] — Birthed

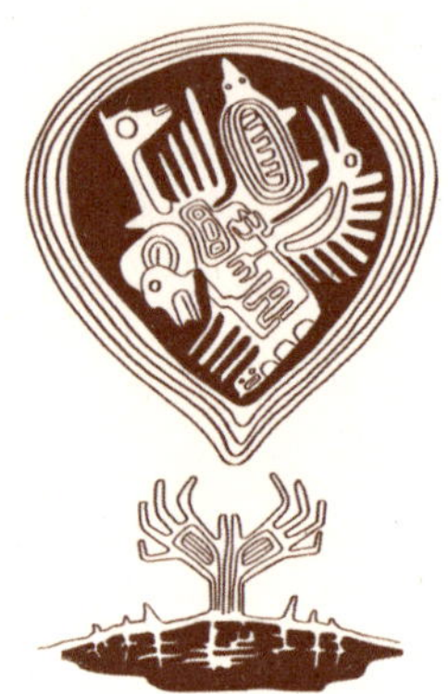

Uqi qarwaqallu wawachastha saktha
Wayaway chullumpi
Qhipatuqur iñakipt´astha
Uqi palumqallu kisjatawi
Wayaway chullumpi

Ch´iyar qarwaqalluy wawachastha saktha
Wayaway chullumpi
Qhipatuqur iñakipt´astha
Chuñakir qallukisjatawi
Wayaway chullumpi

T´axllu qarwaqallu wawachastha saktha
Wayaway chullumpi
Qhipatuqur iñakipt´astha
Puku puk qallukisjatawi
Wayaway chullumpi

46 *Wawachastha saktha*. A newborn llama with the color of a dove.

I gave birth to a lead-colored llama calf, I whispered
Wayaway chullumpi
But when I looked back
It had only been little lead dove
Wayaway chullumpi

I gave birth to a little black-colored llama calf, I whispered
Wayaway chullumpi
But when I looked back,
It had only been a chuñakira[47]
Wayaway chullumpi

I gave birth to a monkey-colored llama calf, I whispered
Wayaway chullumpi
But when I looked back
It had only been a puku puku[48]
Wayaway chullumpi

47 *Chuñakira*. Black bird, symbolizing strength.

48 *Puku puku*. Bird that symbolizes time, hour: the measurer of time. These birds have symbolic meanings like the *Chulumpi* bird that symbolically describes the waves that form in the hair of the llama.

Wanak qalluy wawachastha saktha
Wayawaya chullumpi
Qhipatuqur iñakipt'astha
Wariqallu kisjatawi
Wayaway chullumpi

Paru qarwaqallu wawachastha saktha
Wayaway chullumpi
Qhipatuqur iñakipt'astha
Wikuñqallu kisjatawi
Wayaway chullumpi

I gave birth to a guanaco-colored calf, I whispered
Wayaway chullumpi
But when I looked back,
It had only been a wari child
Wayaway chullumpi

I gave birth to a little golden calf, I whispered
Wayaway chullumpi
But when I looked back,
It had only been a vicuña[49] calf
Wayaway chullumpi

49 *Vicuña*. One of the two wild South American camelids from the high alpine areas of the Andes.

Apas apasma[50]
– Take It Away, Take It Away

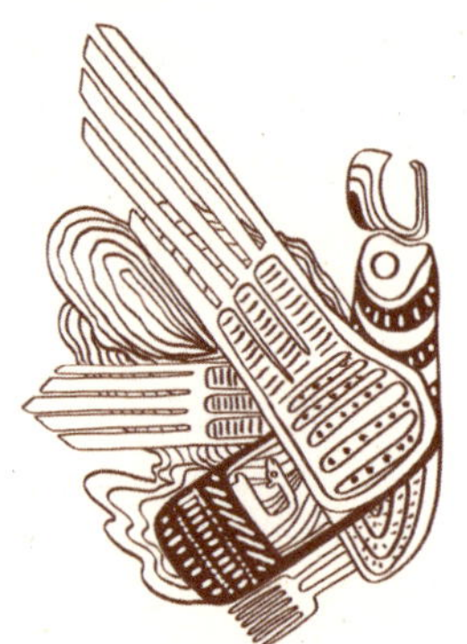

apas apasmay
palumita palumita
saxra qhawañar apasma
palumita palumita
kunay apasintha
palumita palumita
qarwaqalluy apasintha
palumita palumita
panti wistallaniwa
palumita palumita
panti wallqipuniwa
palumita palumita
janiway inatakiti
palumita palumita
janiway q´asitakiti
palumita palumita
awkis taykas sirwiñataki
palumita palumita
jumapiniway taykñata
palumita palumita

50 *Apas apasma*. The cycle of life of the flock, fluctuating up and down like waves.

Take it away, take it away
Little dove, little dove
Take it away in your protective armpit
Little dove, little dove
What did I bring with me
Little dove, little dove
A little llama I brought
Little dove, little dove
It has a feminine cherry-colored bag
Little dove, little dove
He has a masculine cherry-colored bag
Little dove, little dove
It's not in vain
Little dove, little dove
It's not to cry
Little dove, little dove
It is to serve our mothers and fathers
Little dove, little dove
You are my eternal mother
Little dove, little dove

Mamala witay ananta
– Mother of the Eternal Flock

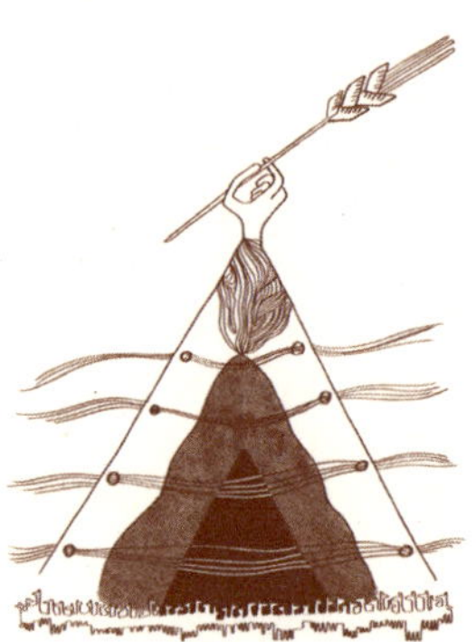

Kawkiy ukar saranta
Mamala wiyay ananta
Alturupiniw saranta
Mamala wiyay ansu
Kunamakiy saranta
Mamala wiyay ananta
Sintakamakiw saranta
Mamala wiyay ansu
Kawkiy ukaru saranta
Mamala wiyay ananta
Pinkillir lumar saranta
Mamala wiyay anasu
Kuna katukam saranta
Mala wiyay ansu
Parway katukan saranta
Mamala wiyay ananta

From where it is you will go
Mother of the eternal flock
Always upwards you will go
Mother of the eternal flock
How will you go
Mother of the eternal flock
Like the ribbon will you go
Mother of the eternal flock
From where it is you always go
Mother of the eternal flock
To the flute hill you will go
Mother of the eternal flock
In search of what you will go
Mother of the eternal flock
You will go fishing for the ear of straw
Mother of the eternal flock

Janiway inatakiti — It Is Not in Vain

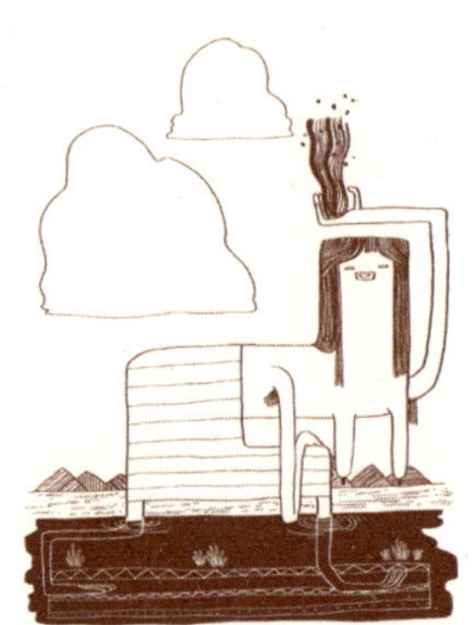

kawkiy ukat ichhtastha
q´asirqutaway ichhtastha
janiway inatakiti
janiway q´asitakiti
kunaruray ichhtastha
panti awayur ichhtastha
janiway inatakiti
janiway q´asitakiti
kunaruray kirt´astha
kastillphant´aruw kirt´astha
janiway inatakiti
janiway q´asitakiti
kunantiray q´awt´astha
apsu q´urawint qawthastha
janiway inatakiti
janiway q´asitakiti

From where did I rise
From Lake Q'asiri I rose
It is not in vain
It's not something to cry about
In what did I rise
In cherry-colored awayu[51] I rose
It's not in vain
It's nothing to cry in,
What I wrapped it in
I wrapped him in a castile blanket.
It's not in vain.
It's not something to cry with,
I'll love him
With a wave of colors I will love him
It is not in vain
It's not to cry

51 *Awayu*. The soul of life that gives fortitude and strength.

Kunakamakiy saranta[52] — What Colors Will You Wear?

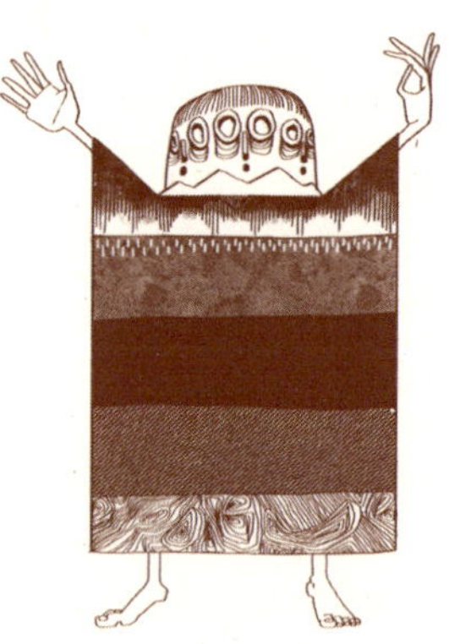

Kunakamakiy saranta
Ch´umphikamakiw saranta
Kunakamakiy saranta
Janq´ukamakiw saranta
Kunakamakiy saranta
Chi´yarkamakiw saranta
Kunakamakiy saranta
Paqukamakiw saranta
Kunakamakiy saranta
T´axllukamakiw saranta
Kunakamakiy saranta
Kunturkamakiw saranta
Kunakamakiy saranta
Wayllatkakiw saranta
Kunakamakiy saranta
Unkhallkamakiw saranta
Kunakamakiy saranta
Parinkamakiw saranta
Kunakamakiy saranta
Pintakamakiw saranta

52 *Saranta*. Color, form and breath. It is also the conjugated verb for *juma* of *saraniña* (to go from over there over here). To walk in different colors and forms.

What colors will you carry?
You will carry brown
What colors will you carry?
You will carry white
What colors do you wear?
You will wear black
What colors will you wear?
You will wear gray
What colors will you wear?
You will wear a stained color
What colors will you wear?
You will go the color of the condor
What colors will you wear?
You will go the color of the of the melanoptera[53]
What colors will you wear?
You will go the color of the duck
What colors will you wear?
You will go the color of the flamingo
What colors will you wear?
You will go beautiful

53 *Melanoptera*. An Andean goose that is white and black with red legs, and rosy bill.

Wayaway tatala[54] —Father Traveler

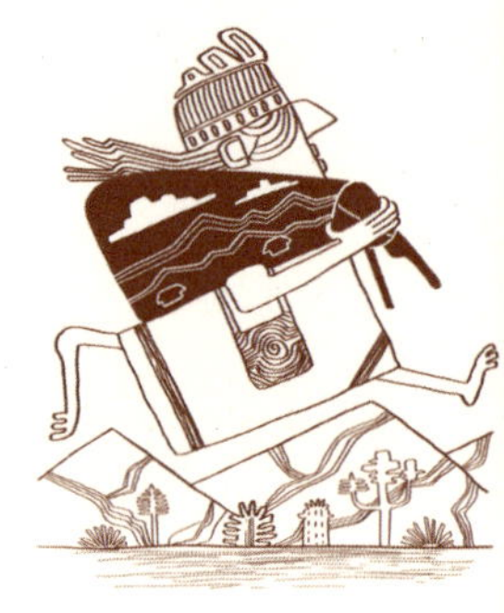

kawkiy ukat saltanta wayaway tatalay
iskinsatway saltantha wayaway tatalay
kawkiy thamay thamanta wayaway tatalay
likin thakiy thamanta wayaway tatalay
kawkiruray thamantanta wayaway tatalay
jan int´at markar thamantanta wayaway tatalay
kawkitrajiy saltaninta wayaway tatalay
aykil markat saltaninta wayaway tatalay
kawkiy ukar saranta wayaway tatalay
jarat jarar saranta wayaway tatalay
jumapiniw awkñata wayaway tatalay
jumapiniw taykñata waway tatalay

54 *Tatala*. Father and señor.

Where will you leave from, father traveler?
From our town you will depart, father traveler?
Where will you walk through, father traveler?
You will walk along the path of the valley, father traveler.
Where will you look out to, father traveler?
You will arrive at an unknown village, father traveler.
Where will you leave from, father traveler?
From the village of Aiquile you will leave, father traveler.
Where will you go to, father traveler?
To a place of rest you will go, father traveler.
You are my eternal father, father traveler.
You are my eternal father, father traveler.

Sikuya panti — The Rhythm of the Siku[55] That Introduces the Verses

qarwanit sakista sikuya apanti
jararankhat qarwani sikuya apanti

ankutanit sakista sikuya apanti
sat´awallut ankutani sikuya apanti

ch´uñunit sakista sikuya apanti
wuru khullamit chuñuni sikuya apanti

jak´unit sakista sikuya apanti
qhillat jak´uni sikuya apanti

ch´ankhullanit sakista sikuya apanti
jararankhat ch´ankhullani sikuya apanti

wiskhanit sakista sikuya apanti
katarit wiskhani sikuya apanti

guitarranit sakista sikuya apanti
wuru palapalat guitarrani sikuya apanti

55 *Siku*. Traditional panpipe, the instrument that introduces the verses.

I have llamas, you tell me, the rhythm of the siku introduces it
You only have lizard llamas, the rhythm of the siku introduces it

I have young llamas, you tell me, the rhythm of the siku introduces it
You only have young llama lizards, the rhythm of the siku introduces it

I have chuño,[56] you tell me, the rhythm of the siku introduces it
You only have donkey dung, the rhythm of the siku introduces it

I have flour, you tell me, the rhythm of the siku introduces it
You only have flour ash, the rhythm of the siku introduces it

I have wool ropes you tell me, the rhythm of the siku introduces it
You only have lizard ropes, the rhythm of the siku introduces it

I have cords, you tell me, the rhythm of the siku introduces it
You only have viper cords, the rhythm of the siku introduces it

I have a guitar, the rhythm of the siku introduces it
You only have a donkey's shoulder blade, the rhythm of the siku introduces it

56 *Chuño*. A dehydrated potato used to cook.

Awtichiri jilata
— Brother of Winter

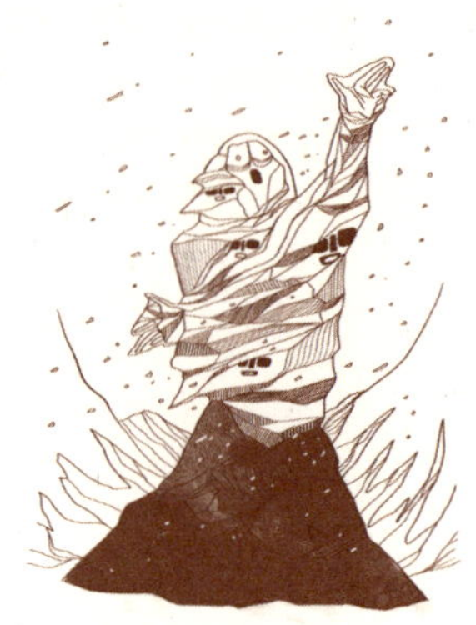

awtichiri jilatay
thayan thaysut jilatay
janiway winknaqañati
jararankhaw manti
awtichiri jilata
thayan thansut jilata
janiway tannaqañati
pakaliway achuri
awtichiri jilata
thayan thaysut jilata
janiway luma lumanak
sarnaqañati atuxaway achuri
awtichiri jilatay
thayan thaysut jilata
jaqhi kunkanak janiway sarnaqañati
kunast ukaw katuri
awtichiri jilata
thayan thaysut jilata

Brother of winter
Frozen by the cold of winter
You don't have to lie there
The lizard knows how to enter
Brother of winter
Frozen by the cold of winter
There is no need to run around
The eagle knows how to carry you
Brother of winter
Frozen by the cold of winter
There is no need to walk through the hills
The fox knows how to carry
Brother of winter
Frozen by the cold of winter
There is no need to walk through the rocks
I don't know what it is, what it knows how to carry
Brother of winter
Frozen by the cold of winter

Mamala paw paw — Eternal Mother Sustainer

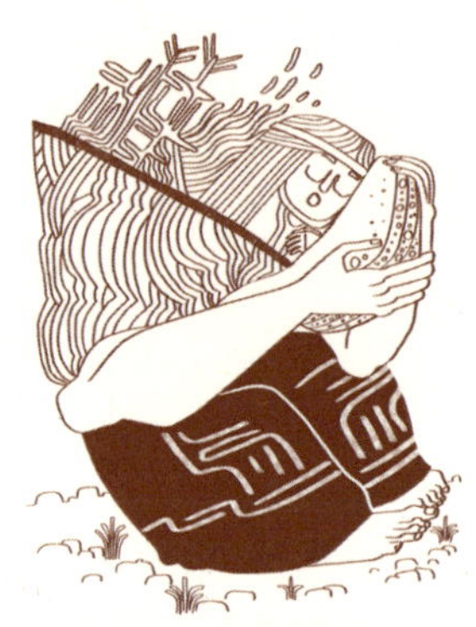

saratmakay saratma mamala paw
paw jaq´u sinta jaquta mamala paw
paw saratmakay saratma mamala
paw paw wila sinta jaquta mamala
paw paw kuna phuqa saranta
mamala paw paw kancha phuqa
saranta mamala paw paw kuna phuqa
saranta mamala paw paw jira phuqa
saranta mamala paw paw janiw
ququt shamati mamala paw paw
janiw wiskhut shamati mamala paw paw
kuna katukam sariri mamala paw paw
parwqay katukam sariri mamala paw paw
kuna katukam sariri mamala paw paw
uma katukam sariri mamala paw paw
kuna sataki mamala paw paw
chita qallu sataki mamala paw paw k
una sataki mamala paw paw
jumapiñay chitata mamala paw paw
pantis t´ikha mamala paw paw
rusas t´ikha mamala paw paw

How pretty you look, mother sustainer
Like a white ribbon stretched out, mother sustainer
How pretty you look, sustaining mother
Like a red ribbon stretched out, sustaining mother
Full of what you will go, sustaining mother
Full of the field you will go, sustaining mother
Full of what, you will go, sustaining mother
Full of strength, you will go, sustaining mother
I'm not going to ask you for lunch, sustaining mother
I'm not going to ask you for sandals, sustaining mother
In search of what, you will go, sustaining mother
In fishing for the ears, you will go, sustaining mother
In search of what, you will go, sustaining mother
In search of water, you will go, sustaining mother
What is your name, sustaining mother
You are called the lamb, sustaining mother
What is your name, sustaining mother
You are the sheep, sustaining mother
Cherry-colored flower, sustaining mother
Rose flower, sustaining mother
Flower of roses, sustaining mother

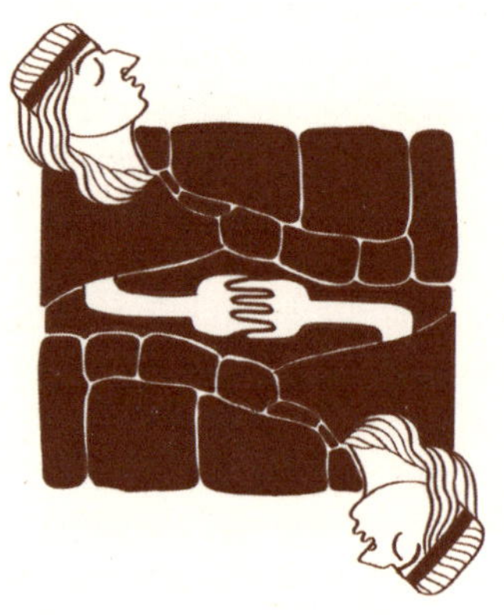

UTACHA KIRKI — CANTO A LA CASA

UTACHA KIRKI — SONG TO THE HOUSE

En el pasado lejano las abuelas y los abuelos contaron a sus nietos que las piedras fueron arreadas por las pastoras y los pastores, a plan de silbato, para construir un pueblo incario.

En esta creación de la poética *utach kirki*, canto a las casas, se centra todos los procesos y procedimientos de construir una casa y un pueblo. Las pastoras y los pastores silbaron desde los cerros más altos para ver donde se dirigirían las piedras, para escoger el lugar perfecto de construcción de una casa y un pueblo incario. En esta ceremonia poética se *ch'allará* al espíritu de las piedras, *qala axayutak umaña*. Las piedras serán cimiento y semilla de esta casa y del pueblo, donde se darán las primeras ofrendas al lugar sagrado de la tierra (*jisk'a iskina* para una casa pequeña, *jach'a iskina* para un pueblo grande). Con las memorias de una estaca del inca, *inka warani*, se unirán las materias primas de distintos lugares, para pedir el permiso a estos seres que acompañarán en la construcción de la casa, *uta*, o un pueblo, *marka*. Se ofrece bebidas y sahumerios a la madera que viene de los valles o del trópico, *llaxlla*, a las pajas duras, *iru wichhu*, que vienen de las alturas y a todos los insumos trasportados por las llamas, *tilantiru*, al lugar perfecto de *inka warani* donde las materias primas son procesadas por el pueblo *wakichaña*. Los hombres moverán las piedras para el cimiento, *inka thaxsin thaxsita*, cementado por los incas y las mujeres desmenuzaran las pajas, *wichhu liq'iña*. Con todo lo desmenuzado se prepara la arcilla *inka ñiq'in kulta*, colada con las arcillas del inca se levanta el muro, *inka pirqan pirqata*, muros construidos por el inca. Finalmente, terminada la estructura de la arquitectura, *inka jiksun jiksuta*, con el acabado perfecto del inca, la estructura de la casa está lista para ser techada. Para el techo se requerirá de la madera *llaxlla* y paja dura, *iru ichhu*, hilos de cuero

In the distant past, grandmothers and grandfathers told their grandchildren that the stones were herded by the shepherds, using a whistle, to build an Incan village.

In this creation of the *utach kirki*[57] poetics, song to the houses, all the processes and procedures of building a house and a village are centered. The shepherds whistled from the highest hills calling the stones down, in dialogue with the stones. The stones choose the perfect place to position themselves as a house and an Incan village. Houses are like people, that also embrace people. An Andean expression is the "embrace of the house" meaning protection from wind and rain. In this poetic ceremony, the spirit of the stones will be called, *qala*[58] *axayutak umaña*. The stones will be the foundation and seed of this house and the town, where the first offerings will be given to the sacred place of the earth. (*jisk'a*[59] *iskina*[60] for a small house, *jach'a*[61] *iskina* for a big village). With the memories of an Inca pole, *inka warani*, raw materials from different places will be united, to ask permission from these beings who will accompany the construction of the house, *uta*, or a village, *marka*. Drinks

57 *Utach kirki*. A term describing how to sing to a house. The song contains the recipe to build a house, including the raw materials to gather, the form, construction and final baptism of a house.

58 *Qala*. A stone related to strength of time, space, and environment.

59 *Jisk'a*. Small.

60 *Iskina*. The sacred place dedicated to offerings in the house, in a community settlement.

61 *Jach'a*. Big.

mat'a para amarrar la unión de las maderas y cordón de paja, *wichhu phala,* para urdir entre las vigas de madera, *turu lawar tilsuña*. Una vez urdidas las sogas de paja se procederá con el orden de las pajas seleccionadas por las mujeres, *wichhu ch'iya*, ordenadas por tamaño de las pajas, grande, mediano y pequeño que sería *jach'a much'u, tantiy much'u y jisk'a much'u*. Las pajas grandes *jach'a much'u* entrarán en todos los bordes inferiores del techo y siguiendo con las pajas medianas y pequeñas en la parte central. El final del techo también se terminará con pajas medianas y grandes para poder cubrir de la mejor manera. Una vez terminado el techado de la casa, comienza la ceremonia con las mejores poéticas de la memoria de una construcción de la casa, comenzando con los cantos de las materia primas, de cómo se trasladaron al lugar. Se realiza una ceremonia dedicada a los *axayu* de las materias primas, para pedir el máximo apoyo para esa construcción de un ser nuevo de la familia, la casa, *uta*, o un pueblo, *marka*. También ofrendas al cimiento de la casa y un pueblo, *taxsi*, siguiendo con el proceso de las paredes, *pirqa*, y finalmente el techado, *utachaña*. Todos estos versos de la poética serán combinados principalmente por las mujeres y luego por los hombres. Mientras aflore la poética de la memoria llegan las tías con las ofrendas de semillas de cereales, tubérculos y pelos de animales, que se llama *jatha pirwa, muju pirwa y uywa pirwa* que será recibidos con mucho cariño y afecto por los familiares. Finalmente, llega la hora perfecta para los cantos de un bautizo o una *ch'alla*: a media noche se da lugar un performance que presenta a el inka cura, quien llega a bautizar la casa y el pueblo. Las niñas y niños del pueblo son los más entusiasmados, pues además de conocer al inca cura, al pasar las horas de la noche se irán integrando junto al pueblo a este performance. Los cantos

and incense are offered to the wood that comes from the valleys or the tropic, *llaxlla*, to the hard straws, *iru wichhu*, that come from the heigh altitudes and to all the supplies transported by the llamas, *tilantiru,*[62] to the perfect place of Incan constellation where raw materials are processed by the people *wakichaña.*[63] The men will move the stones for the foundation, *inka thaxsin thaxsita*, cemented by the Inca, and the women will break up the straw, *wichhu*[64] *liq'iña.*[65] Walls are built by the Inca: with everything crumbled, the Inca clay, *ñiq'in kulta,* is prepared, cast with the Inca clays the wall is raised, *inka pirqan pirqata.*[66] Finally, with the architectural structure finished, *inka jiksun jiksuta*, with the perfect finish of the Inca, the structure of the house is ready to be roofed. For the roof, *llaxlla*[67] wood and *iru ichhu,* hard straw, will be required. To tie the union of wood and straw, *mat'a*[68] leather threads and *wichhu phala,* straw cords, weave between the wooden beams, *turu lawar tilsuña*. Once the straw ropes have been woven, the order of the straws selected by the women will proceed,

62 *Tilantiru*. The llama that guides the way through the valleys.

63 *Wakichaña*. To prepare, to get ready.

64 *Wichhu*. Straw.

65 *Liq'iña*. To hit, hammer or knock.

66 *Pirqata*. Stone walls built with arduous work to delineate fields and roads; for the cultivation of terraces and retention of water; and protection of infrastructure benefiting people and animals.

67 *Llaxlla*. Wood that comes from lowlands.

68 *Mat'a*. Rope made from leather, leather thread to tie the wood to make a house.

seguirán hasta unirse al sonido del bombo *bum, bum, bum*, que abre el camino para que el inca cura pueda ir pasando de una a otra casa nueva.

El inca será recibido con bebidas y comidas de la noche para que pueda disfrutar y celebrar estas nuevas construcciones, él procederá a hacer las *ch'alla* más grandes de la noche con sahumerios de yerbas aromáticas y ofrendas de bebidas para todas las casas nuevas y el pueblo nuevo. Gracias a las ofrendas del inca, el pueblo entero celebrará con poéticas más profundas que se traducen en rondas o *wayñu* que florecen dando lugar al *wayñu wayñuña*.

wichhu ch'iya, ordered by size of the straws, large, medium and small, called *jach'a much'u, tantiy*[69] *much'u* and *jisk'a much'u*. The large *jach'a much'u* straws will enter all the lower borders of the roof and continue with the medium and small straws in the central part. The ends of the roof will also be finished with medium and large straws to provide the best coverage. Once the roofing of the house is finished, the ceremony begins with the best memetic poetics of the construction of a house, beginning with the songs of raw materials, and of how they were moved to the place. A ceremony is held dedicated to the *axayu*[70] of raw materials, to ask for maximum support for the construction of a new member of the family, the house, *uta*, or town, *marka*. Also, offerings to the foundation of the house and a town, *taxsi*, continuing with the process of the walls, *pirqa*, and finally the roof, *utachaña*. All these poetic verses will be combined at first by women and then by men. While memetic poetics flourish, aunts arrive with offerings of cereals, tubers and animal furs, which are called *jatha pirwa, muju pirwa* and *uywa pirwa*, which will be received with great love and affection by family members. Finally, the perfect moment arrives for the songs of a baptism or a *ch'alla:*[71] at midnight a performance takes place that presents the Inca priest, who arrives to bless the house and the town. The girls and boys of the town are the most enthusiastic, because in addition

69 *Tantiy*. Medium sized.

70 *Axayu*. The soul of life that gives fortitude and strength. It is omnipresent and eternally present in all things: plants, animals, and the earth itself.

71 *Ch'alla*. An opening or closing ceremony, libation in honor of Pachamama. *Ch'alla* is also sand and a sandy area.

to meeting the Inca priest, as the hours of the night pass, they will join the town in this performance. The songs will continue until they join the sound of the drum, *boom, boom, boom* opening the way for the Inca priest to move from one new house to another.

The Inca will be received with drinks and meals at night so that he can enjoy and celebrate these new constructions. He will proceed to make the largest *ch'alla* of the night with aromatic herb incense and offerings of drinks for all the new houses and the new town. Thanks to the Inca's offerings, the entire town will celebrate with deepest poetics that are translated into rounds or *wayñu* that flourish giving rise to the *wayñu wayñuña*.[72]

72 *Wayñu*. A type of folk-tune and dance in couples.

Inkay
— Incay

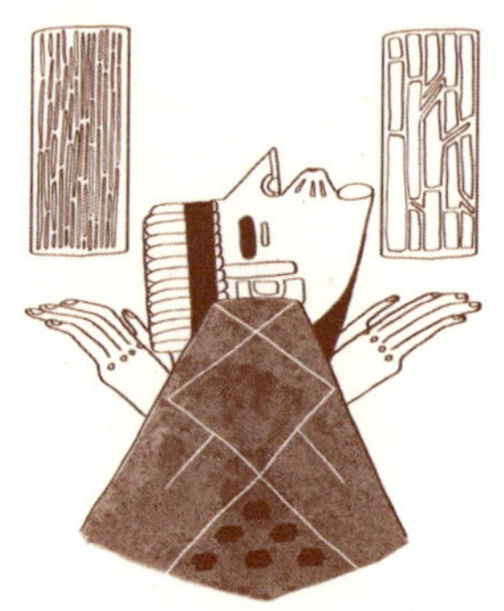

Kunarakiy juthanji Inkay
tilantiruw juthanji Inkay
Kawkiranat juthanji Inkay
patxaranat juthanji Inkay

Kuna kallaw juthanji Inkay
wichu kallaw juthanji
Iñaki Kaw kiranat juthanji Inkay
patxaranat juthanji inkay

Kuna kallaw juthanji Inkay
llaxlla kallaw juthanji Inkay
Kawkiranat juthanji Inkay
manqharanat juthanji inkay

Kawkiruray juthanji Inkay
taypiranar juthanji inkay
Kunaruray juthanji inkay
machaq mark amir juthanji Inkay

What is coming, Incay?
The leader comes Incay
From where does it come, Incay?
From the highest part it comes Incay

Loaded with what does it come, Incay?
Loaded with straw it comes Incay
Where does it come from, Incay?
From the highest part it comes Incay

Load of what is it coming, Incay?
Load of wood comes Incay
From where does it come, Incay?
From the lowest part it comes Incay

From where are you coming, Incay?
To the center is coming Incay
To what is coming, Incay?
To build a new town is coming Incay

Siw siw inkay[73] — Says and Says Incay

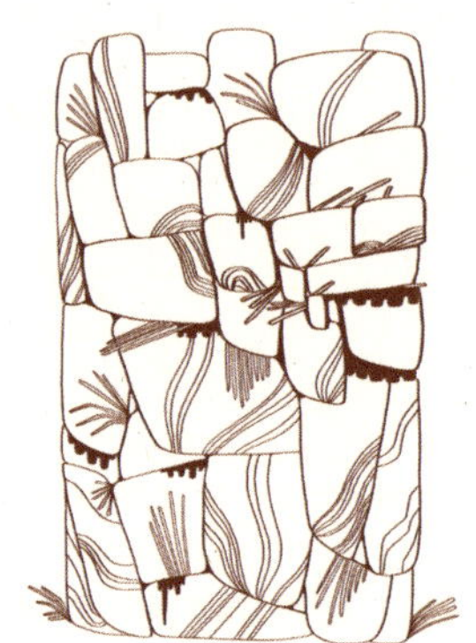

Kuna thaxsin thaxsita siw siw Inkay
Inka thaxsin thaxsita siw siw Inkay
Kuna qalan thaxsita siw siw Inkay
Iinka qalan thaxsita siw siw Inkay
Kuna pirqan pirqata siw siw Inkay
Inka pirqan pirqata siw siw Inkay
Kuna kulan kula siw siw Inkay
Inka kula kulata siw siw Inkay
Kuna jiksun jiksuta siw siw Inkay
Inka jiksun jiksuta siw siw Inkay
Kuna ch'ijmat ch'ijmaniw siw siw Inkay
Inka wayllat ch'ijmani siw siw Inkay
Kuna chhaxllat chhaxllani siw siw Inkay
Inka chhaxllat chhaxllani siw siw Inkay
Kuna q'awan q'awata siw siw Inkay
Inka q'awan q'awata siw siw Inkay
Kuna wichhut wichhuni siw siw Inkay
Inka wichhut wichhuni siw siw Inkay
Kuna thaphan thaphachata siw siw
Inkay Inka thapan thaphachata siw siw Inkay

73 The instruction of the Inca. The Inca ceremony brings the knowledge of construction and engineering.

Cemented by who, says and says Incay
Cemented by the Incas, says and says Incay
With what stone is it cemented, says and says Incay
With stone from the Incas, says and says Incay
By whom is the wall built, says and says Incay
Built by the Incas, says and says Incay
With what clay is it glued, says and says Incay
With Inca clay, says and says Incay
With what finish is it finished, says and says Incay
With the finish of the Inca it is finished, says and says Incay
With what support is it supported, says and says Incay
With the support of straw of the Inca, says and says Incay
Wood of whom it has, says and says Incay
Wood of the Inca, says and says Incay
With what wrapping is it wrapped, says and says Incay
With the wrapping of the Inca, says and says Incay
Straws of whom it has, says and says Incay
Straws of the Inca it has, says and says Incay
By whom is the nest built, says and says Incay
The nest is built by the Incas, says and says Incay

Chiru chiru[74] — Chiru Chiru

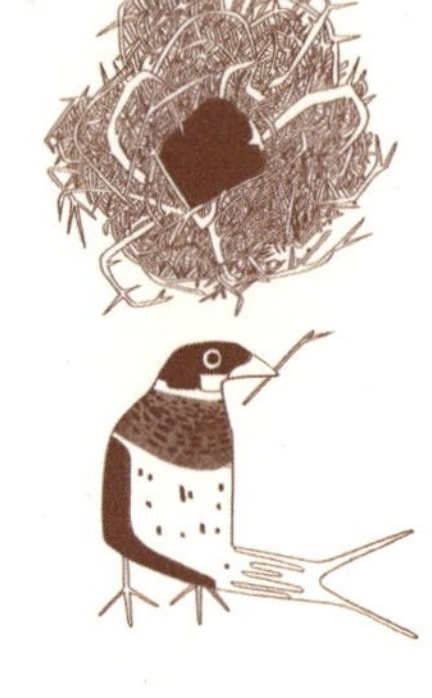

Thapach thapachma chiru chiru
Alturupiniw thapachanta chiru chiru
Ayilira juthanispa chiru chiru
Pakalira juthanispa chiru chiru
Alturupiniw thapachanta chiru chiru

Thapach thapachma chiru chiru
Warancurupiniw thapachanta chiru chiri
Ayilira juthanispa chiru chiru
Pakalira juthanispa chiru chiru
Alturupiniw thapachanta chiru chruiru

Thapach thapachma chiru chiru
Alturupiniw thapachanta chiru chiru
Ayilira juthanispa chiru chiru
Pakalira juthanispa chiru chiru
Alturupiniw thapachanta chiru chiru

74 *Chiru*. A bird that constructs its house in the highest parts, built in a large round ball shape, in a way that the nest is so strong and well-built it is inherited by future generations of birds.

Build, build, Chiru Chiru
Certainly, at the highest point, Chiru Chiru
Watch out the eagle could come Chiru Chiru
Watch out the hawk comes, Chiru Chiru
Certainly build at the highest point, Chiru Chiru

Build, build, Chiru Chiru
Certainly, in the ravine part, Chiru Chiru
Watch out the eagle comes, Chiru Chiru
Watch out the hawk comes, Chiru Chiru
Build at the highest point, Chiru Chiru

Build, build, Chiru Chiru
At the highest point, Chiru Chiru
Watch out the eagle comes, Chiru Chiru
Watch out the hawk comes, Chiru Chiru
Build at the highest point, Chiru Chiru

Kuntur mamani
— Señora Condor

Kuna kulat kulani kutur mamani
ñiq'i kulat kulani kuntur mamani
Wayñuy wayñuy kuntur mamani
Wayñuy wayñu kuntur mamani

Kuna pirqat pirqani kuntur mamani
atup asukarat pirqani kuntur mamani
Wayñuy wayñuy kuntur mamani
Wayñuy wayñuy kuntur mamani

Kuna ch'ijmat ch'ijmani kuntur mamani
wichhu ch'ijmat ch'ijmani kuntur mamani
Wayñuy wayñuy kuntur mamani
Wayñuy wayñuy kuntur mamani

Tail of what do you have Condor
Clay tail you have Condor
Dance, dance Condor
Dance, dance Condor

Walls of what do you have Condor
Sugar adobe wall Condor
Dance, dance Condor
Dance, dance Condor

Pillow of what do you have Condor
Pillow of straw you have Condor
Dance, dance Condor
Dance, dance Condor

Sinsiy[75]
— Pulse

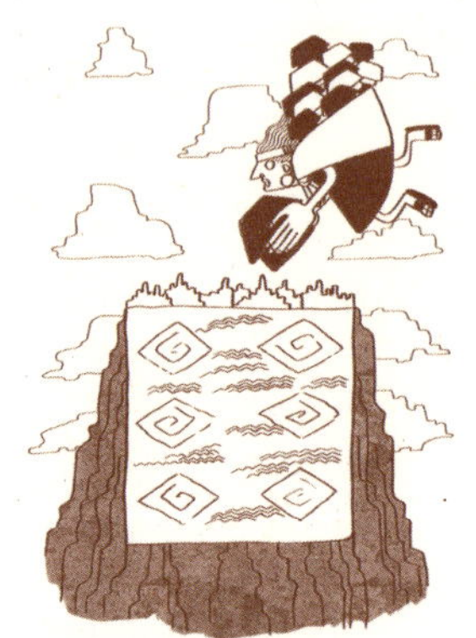

Kunarakiy juthanji Sinsiy
Inka kuraw juthanji Sinsiy
Kawkitrajiy juthanji Sinsiy
Qhusqhu markat juthanji Sinsiy
Kunarakiy juthanji Sinsiy
Inka kuraw juthanji Sinsiy
Kawkitrajiy juthanji Sinsiy
Putusitway juthanji Sinsiy
Kunaruray juthanji Sinsiy
Machaq mark armasjipana Sinsiy
Inka kuraw juthanji Sinsiy
Iskinaruw juthanji Sinsiy
Thaxsinuqir juthanji Sinsiy
Ut´ayiriw juthanji Sinsiy
Marckachiriw juthanji Sinsiy
Juthanjiway juthanji Sinsiy
Inka kuraw juthanji Sinsiy

75 *Sinsiy*. The pulse, rhythm that helps the heart beats to flow in different ways.

What is it that is coming, Sinsiy?
The Inca priest is coming, Sinsiy
From where is he coming, Sinsiy?
From Cusco he is coming, Sinsiy
For what is he coming, Sinsiy?
The Inca priest is coming, Sinsiy
From where is he coming, Sinsiy?
From Potosí he is coming, Sinsiy
For what is he coming, Sinsiy?
To arm a new town, Sinsiy
The Inca priest is coming, Sinsiy?
To our place is he coming, Sinsiy
To cement is he coming, Sinsiy?
To settle he is coming, Sinsiy
To settle is he coming, Sinsiy?
Comes and comes, Sinsiy
The Inca priest is coming, Sinsiy

Pantis mik´illu murarus mik´illu[76] — Pantis mik´illu

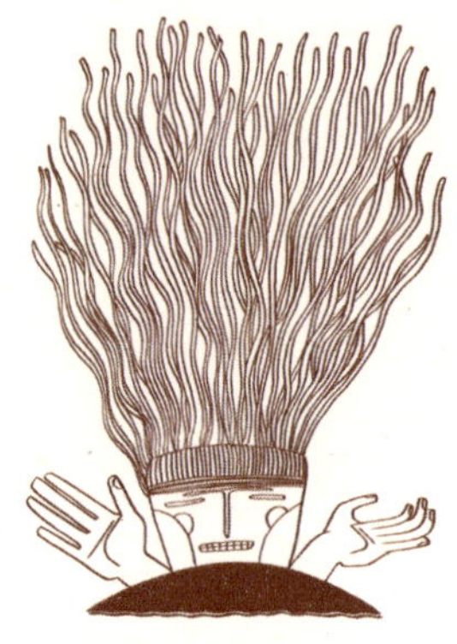

Juthan juthanpa
pantis mik´illu murarus mik´illu
Wira quchas juthanpa
pantis mik´íllu murarus muk´íllu

Juthan juthanpa
pantis mikillu murarus mik´íllu
Khistis kawkis juthanpa
pantis mik´illu murarus mik´illu

Juthan juthanpa
pantis mik´illu murarus mik´illu
Ukatakiy wustutawa
pantis mik´íllu murarus muk´íllu

Juthan juthanpa
pantis mik´illu murarus mik´illu
Kuna kastas juthanpa
pantis mik´illu murarus mik´illu

76 *Murarus mik´illu*. The transformation of color and form in a flower from bud to bloom.

Let it come and let it come
pantis mik´íllu murarus mik´íllu
Even if it is the wira qucha,[77] let it come
pantis mik´íllu murarus mik´íllu

Let it come and let it come
pantis mik ´íllu murarus mik ´íllu
Whoever it is, let it come
pantis mik ´íllu murarus mik ´íllu

Let it come and let it come
pantis mik ´íllu murarus mik ´íllu
For that I am ready
pantis mik´íllu murarus mik´íllu

Let it come and let it come
pantis mik ´íllu murarus mik ´íllu
Of any kind, let it come
pantis mik ´íllu murarus mik ´íllu

77 *Wira qucha*. An eternal Señor with a robust, round form. This also alludes to the Andean deity, Wiraqucha.

Juthan juthanpa
pantis mik'illu murarus mik'illu
Jiwasaway wustutanwa
pantis mik'illu murarus mik'illu

Juthan juthanpa
pantis mik'illu murarus mikillu
Wira quchas juthanpan
pantis mikillu murarus mikillu

Let it come and let it come
pantis mik ´íllu murarus mik ´íllu
For that we are both ready
pantis mik´íllu murarus mik´íllu

Let it come and let it come
pantis mik´íllu murarus mik´íllu
Even if it is the wira qucha, let it come
pantis mik´íllu murarus mik´íllu

Si inkay
—If Incay Says Incay

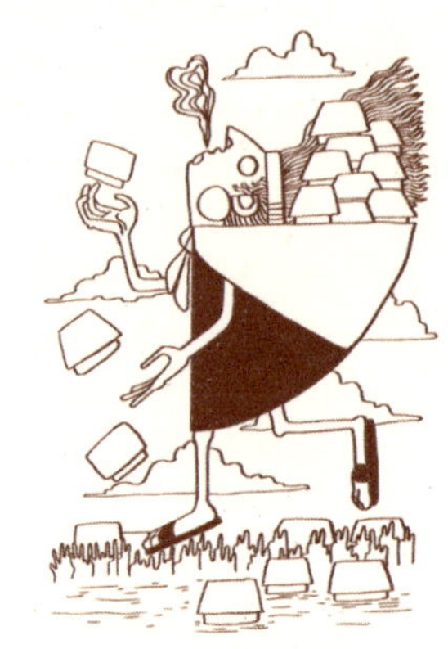

Inka kuraw juthanji si Inkay
Kawkiy ukat juthanji si Inkay

Machaq mark armasjipana si Inkay
Tata kuraw juthanji si Inkay

Chukiyawut juthanji si Inkay
Tamput tampur juthanji si Inkay

Liwanjit liwanjir juthanji si Inkay
Machaq mark armasjipana si Inkay

Kunatrajiy juthanji si Inkay
Markatakiw juthanji si Inkay

Kawkirakiy thaxsi si Inkay
Machaq mark armasjipanna si Inkay

Tata kuraw juthanji si inkay
Tamput tampur juthanji si Inkay

Liwanjut liwanjur juthanji si Inkay
Tata kuraw juthanji si Inkay
Apuray justuchasjanta si Inkay

The Inca priest is coming, says Incay
Where is he coming from? says Incay

When a new village is being built, says Incay
The priest is coming, says Incay

From Chuquiago he comes, says Incay
Tambo by tambo[78] he is coming, says Incay

Kilometer by kilometer he is coming, says Incay
When a village is arming itself, says Incay

Why is he coming? says Incay
To see the new village he is coming, says Incay

Where is the foundation? says Incay
When the new village is being armed, says Incay

The priest is coming, says Incay
Tambo by tambo he is coming, says Incay

Kilometer by kilometer he is coming, says Incay
The priest is coming, says Incay
Hurry up and get ready, says Incay

78 *Tambo*. A location suitable for hosting people and exchanging food products, animals, and information. The contemporary notion of tambo is a market.

Chinchilla[79] — Chinchilla

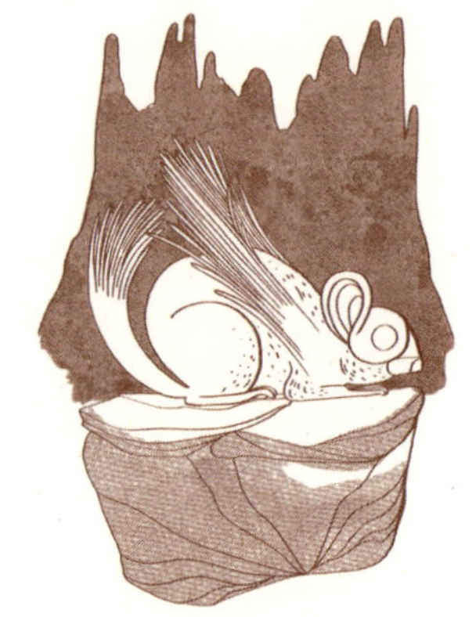

Irpay irpay chinchilla
Wayñuy wayñuy chinchilla
Irpay irpay chinchilla
Wayñuy wayñuy chinchilla
Kuna alat alani chinchilla
Wichhu alat alani chinchilla
Irpay irpay chinchilla
Wayñuy wayñuy chinchilla
Irpay irpay chinchilla
Wayñuy wayñuy chinchilla
Kuna k´anat k´anani chinchilla
Wichhu k´anat k´anani chinchilla
Irpay irpay chinchilla
Wayñuy wayñuy chinchilla
Irpay irpay chinchilla
Wayñuy wayñuy chinchilla
Kuna wich´inkhata wichinkhani chinchilla
Wichhu wichinkhat wich´inkhani chilla
Irpay irpay chinchilla
Wayñuy wayñuy chinchilla
Irpay irpay chinchilla
Wayñuy wayñuy chinchilla

79 *Chinchilla*. A small mammal native to the Andes, also meaning a very fine and brilliant coat. The silk of the Andes.

Guide and guide, Chinchilla
Dance, dance, Chinchilla
Guide and guide, Chinchilla
Dance, dance, Chinchilla
Wings of what do you have, Chinchilla
Wings of straw do you have, Chinchilla
Guide and guide, Chinchilla
Dance, dance, Chinchilla
Guide and guide, Chinchilla
Dance, dance, Chinchilla
Braids of what do you have, Chinchilla
Braids of straw do you have, Chinchilla
Guide and guide, Chinchilla
Dance, dance, Chinchilla
Guide and guide, Chinchilla
Dance, dance, Chinchilla
Tail of what do you have, Chinchilla
Tail of straw do you have, Chinchilla
Guide and guide, Chinchilla
Dance, dance, Chinchilla
Guide and guide, Chinchilla
Dance, dance, Chinchilla

palaway juthanji inkay[80] — The Aunt is Coming, Incay

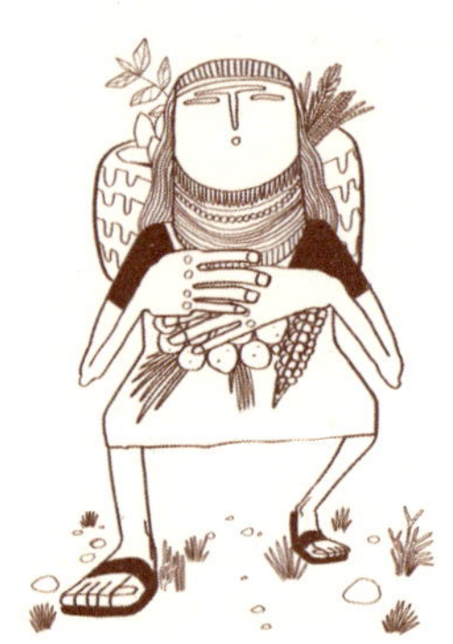

Ipalaway juthanji Inkay
Kunray ipala apanji Inkay
Ipala taqi chayi q´ipiw juthanji Inkay
Pirwa t´allaw juthanji Inkay
Pirwa parwayuw juthanji Inkay

Ipataway juthanji Inkay
Kunray ipata q´ipinji Inkay
Taqi chayiway q´ipinji Inkay
Ipataway q´ipinji Inkay
Tunkapan piluy apanji Inkay

Ukapiniw ut thaxst´ayani Inkay
Ipataway thaxst´ayani Inkay
Taqi chajintiw thaxs´ayani Inkay
Juphapiniw thaxst´ayani Inkay

80 The house is finished, and the aunt comes to offer container of sacred flowers to declare it ready, that nothing will be missing. The aunt is thanked with food and gifts.

The aunt is coming, Incay
What is it that she is bringing? Incay
The aunt is bringing all the spirits of the seeds, Incay
Storehouse of tubers she brings, Incay
Storehouse of cereals she brings, Incay

The aunt is coming, Incay
The aunt comes loading what? Incay
The spirits of the animals and plants she brings, Incay
The aunt is loading, Incay
The twelve hairs is she bringing, Incay

She will cement the house, Incay
The aunt has to cement the house, Incay
With all the products she has to cement, Incay
Only she has to cement, Incay

Wayñu Mikayla[81] — The Verses of Mikayla

Musan musanma wayñu Mikayla
Mayatrajiy musanma wayñu kukusa

Musan musanma wayñu Mikayla
Mayatrajiy musanma wayñu kukusa
Machaq mark armasjipana wayñu wayñuña
Machaq mark armasjipana waynu wayñuña

Wayñuy wayñuy wayñu Mikayla
Wayñuy wayñuy wayñu kukusa

Musan musanma wayñu Mikayla
Mayatrajiy musanma wayñu kukusa
Musan musanma wayñu Mikayla
Mayatrajiy musanma wayñu kukusa

81 As one combines colors one also combines verses.

Combine, combine verses, Mikayla
One by onc your verses, Mikayla

Combine, combine verses, Mikayla
One by one your verses, Mikayla
When a town is arming itself, one must dance
When a town is arming itself, one must dance

Dance, dance your verses, Mikayla
Dance, dance your verses, Mikayla

Combine, combine verses, Mikayla
One by one your verses of, Mikayla
Combine, combine verses of, Mikayla
One by one your verses, Mikayla

Palantata palantata — Sprout Sprout

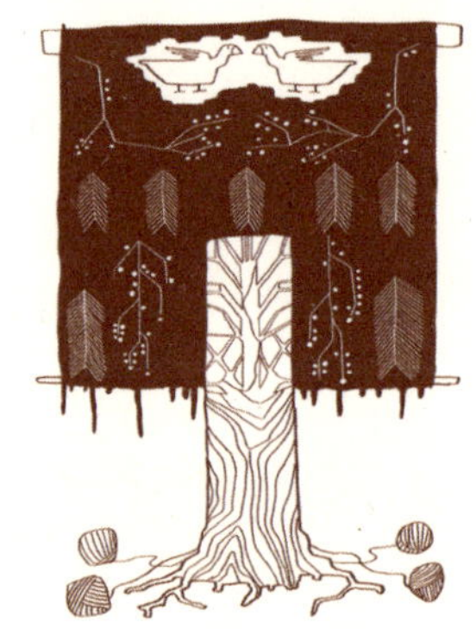

masuruy ch´ulla paloma
jichhuruy paris paloma
azucenay azucena
jawkha suma azucena
kawkirakiy ipata
kawkirakiy tiyula
ina k´anacha k´antjañani
apsu k´anach k´antjañani

kawkirakiy ipata
kawkirakiy tiyula
ina qatach qatjañani
apsu qatach qatjañani
palantatay palantata
jawkha sumay palanta
aliy aliy alisjanta
mulli aliy alisjanta

palantatay palantata
jawkha sumay palanta
tukuspana tukuspana
wara miryar tukuspana

Yesterday only a single dove
Today a pair of doves
Lily and lily
What lovely lilies
Where is the aunt?
Where is the uncle?
Shall we weave the normal braid
Or shall we weave the complex braid?

Where is the tiya?[82]
Where is the tiyo?
Shall we weave the normal braid
Or shall we weave the complex braid?
Planted and planted
It is very well planted
It will always be growing
Like the peppertree

Planted and planted
It is very well planted
Let it end, let it end
At the tip of the stick let it end

82 Between the *tiya* (aunt) and *tiyo* (uncle) the house is woven, and the family is woven.

GLOSSARY

AYMARA - ENGLISH

Apas apasma. The cycle of life of the flock, fluctuating up and down like waves.

Aruray. To greet, to salute, and to communicate via a medium.

Awayu. A traditional hand-woven cloth from the Andes used to carry food, babies and other important things, it is also used as a cover blanket for comfort and warmth.

Axayu. The soul of life that gives fortitude and strength. It is omnipresent and eternally present in all things: plants, animals, and the earth itself.

Ch'alla. An opening or closing ceremony, libation in honor of Pachamama. Ch'alla is also sand and a sandy area.

Chana chana. Sacred flower from the valley used in carnival.

Chiru. A bird that constructs its house in the highest parts, built in a large round ball shape, in a way that the nest is so strong and well-built it is inherited by future generations of birds.

Chuca Cuma. A fragrant and branchy plant that is used by indigenous populations to treat altitude sickness, stomach pain and other ailments.

Chullumpi. Grebe. Waves made in a lake by the grebe. A mythological Andean bird that also poetically describes the waves that form in the long hair of the llama when the wind blows.

Chinchilla. A small mammal native to the Andes, also meaning a very fine and brilliant coat. The silk of the Andes.

Chuñakira. Black bird, symbolizing strength.

Chuño. A dehydrated potato used to cook.

Chuwas. A small clay dish in which you put a candle to shine, giving light.

Irpa. The one who leads. Irpa Irpa is the one who guides the flocks through paths with bravery and valor in the best way possible.

Iskina. The sacred place dedicated to offerings in the house, in a community settlement.

Jach'a. Big.

Jisk'a. Small.

Jujchu t'alla. A sacred female protector hill that cares for the inhabitants of the area.

Llaxlla. Wood that comes from lowlands.

Liq'iña. To hit, hammer or knock.

Mat'a. Rope made from leather, leather thread to tie the wood to make a house.

Melanoptera. An Andean goose that is white and black with red legs, and rosy bill.

Minka. An Andean tradition of community work that is carried out to help everyone. The word minka comes from the Quechua minccacuni, which means "to ask for help by promising something." It is a practice that seeks to synthesize relationships of reciprocity. In the minka, community members come together to work on a common goal, such as building a house or harvesting a crop.

Murarus mik'illu. The transformation of color and form in a flower from bud to bloom.

Niña k'ara. A bird with fire sparks. According to the stories it is a nocturnal bird. A secondary meaning of niña k'ara is a person transporting fire in a clay vessel.

Phanchay liryusa. Blooming lilies, also symbolizing opening one's heart, space, mind, and soul.

Phuju. A crystal-clear spring or pool with magical powers of nourishment.

Pirqata. Stone walls built with arduous work to delineate fields and roads; for the cultivation of terraces and retention of water; and protection of infrastructure benefiting people and animals.

Pirwa. A large community storage place for the storage and distribution of resources such as food and textiles.

Pukara. A protective deity. A sacred hill, guardian, protector and creator. A place that protects its inhabitants.

Puku puku. A bird symbolizing the hour; the measurer of time.

Puluy. Implies multiple meanings including the umbilical cord, human and textile, belly, abdomen, and bowels. It is also the belly button, the breath that creates life, further representing femininity. An instrument made from a hollowed-out gourd. The name puluy puluy puluy imitates the sound of this instrument linguistically.

Purta. A place where only male llamas can live.

Putu putu. A sacred red flower from the valley only used for special offerings.

Qala. A stone related to strength of time, space, and environment.

Qarwa phaqhara. Earrings for llamas. Qarwa is llama and phaqhara is flower.

Qarwa sinsiru. A bell that llamas wear on their collar, its ring symbolically opens new spaces and paths.

Qhañi. Refers to a container for textiles, a pouch, a portable sewing bag. In this book it also contains verses. It is a metaphor for a song that contains verses with information as a mnemonic tool.

Quispi. To illuminate the life of someone or something, awakening the spirit or the soul.

Salwi. A joining of the Catholic concept of salvation with the Aymara traditional herb of healing.

Sami. The word has multiple interwoven meanings referring to life essence such as color, luck, destiny, and breath. Color, breath, life (because through breathing life is possible), and air: the air that fills the lungs to live. Forces of life, sami also refers to the door to the state of life.

Saranta. Color, form and breath. It is also the conjugated verb for juma of saraniña (to go from over there over here). To walk in different colors and forms.

Señora/Virgen Dolores. (Spanish). Partially a Catholic appropriation, this concept developed to symbolize the integration of the Catholic and the Aymara community. The Virgin Mary transforms into Pachamama, or Mother earth, sick from the exploitation of the land in Potosí.

Siku. Traditional panpipe, the instrument that introduces the verses.

Sinsiy. The pulse, rhythm that helps the heart beats to flow in different ways.

Simay maya. Songs sung once per week.

Sirkuy. A resting place for those who are alive and those who are resting after death.

Tatala. Father and señor.

Tama. Herd, also a numerous family moving in unity.

Tambo. A location suitable for hosting people and exchanging food products, animals, and information. The contemporary notion of tambo is a market.

Tani tani. Sacred flowers used in ceremonies, grown in high, middle, and low elevations.

Tantiy. Medium sized.

Tilantiru. The llama that guides the way through the valleys.

Tiya/tiyo. Aunt and uncle.

Tupuraya is **pukara**, or **uywiri**, a sacred, protective hill: a place that protects its inhabitants, from the Pukina language.

Turu mallku. A sacred male protector hill that cares for the inhabitants of the area.

Uma. Water, the primordial liquid flowing in our bodies, in space, in the land, and in time.

Untu. Fat or suet, usually from llama, used as an offering or as medicine.

Urqu. Male llama, selected to guide the baby male llamas.

Urusisa. A full day of celebration, a day of festivity, the best day of celebration, where the community gathers, talks, and enjoys the abundance of the new harvest. Uru is Quechua, sisa is Aymara, so the word itself is a joining of Quechua and Aymara with the Catholic day of Easter.

Utach kirki. A term describing how to sing to a house. The song contains the recipe to build a house, including the raw materials to gather, the form, construction and final baptism of a house.

Uywaña. To nurture or to rear mutually and let oneself be reared; to mutually educate and protect.

Uywiri. A mountain deity, sacred hill, guardian, protector and creator. It translates directly as nurturer, or the one who nurtures. It is also referred to as a place that protects its inhabitants.

Vicuña. One of the two wild South American camelids from the high alpine areas of the Andes.

Wakichaña. To prepare, to get ready.

Wichhu ch'iya. A tie made from straws to make a house.

Wayñu. A type of folk-tune and couple dance.

Wawachastha saktha. A newborn llama with the color of a dove.

Wira qucha. An eternal Señor with a robust, round form. This also alludes to the Andean deity, Wiraqucha.

Yuru. A medium sized jug used normally to carry liquids such as water or ceremonial drinks such as Chicha. It is used in offerings.

INCA Press
http://incapress.org/

editions:

Forms of Education:
Couldn't Get a Sense of It
2016

Free as in Free...
2016

To Make a Public:
Temporary Art Review 2011-2016
2017

manuel arturo abreu:
Incalculable Loss
2018

Aeron Bergman and Alejandra Salinas:
Telepathy 传心术
2018

Aeron Bergman and Alejandra Salinas:
Contra el Bien General
2022

Elvira Espejo Ayca:
KIRKI QHAÑI / CONTAINER OF ANDEAN POETICS
2025

COLOPHON

Elvira Espejo Ayca
KIRKI QHAÑI
CONTAINER OF ANDEAN POETICS

PUBLISHED BY
INCA Press

PRINT
Kerschoffset, Zagreb 2025

ISBN
978-0-9977639-6-6

PRINT RUN
750

EDITORS AND TRANSLATORS
Alejandra Salinas, Aeron Bergman, Elvira Espejo Ayca

TRANSLATION REVISION
Adrian Alarcón

DRAWINGS
Salvador Pomar

DESIGNER
Rafaela Drazic

The Spanish Translation of this book titled KIRKI QHAÑI / Petaca De Las Poéticas Andinas, by Elvira Espejo Ayca, was published by El Cuervo Editorial in La Paz, Bolivia in 2022

With support from the Buddy Taub Foundation, Los Angeles